FTCE Elementary Education K-6 Study Guide 2024-2025

Unlock Success with Detailed Coverage of Language Arts, Math, Science, Social Studies – FTCE K-6 Teacher Certification Exam Resources and Full-Length Practice Tests

Test Treasure Publication

Copyright

All content, materials, and publications available on this website and through Test Treasure Publication's products, including but not limited to, study guides, flashcards, online materials, videos, graphics, logos, and text, are the property of Test Treasure Publication and are protected by United States and international copyright laws.

Copyright © 2024-2025 Test Treasure Publication. All rights reserved.

No part of these publications may be reproduced, distributed, or transmitted in any form or by any means, including photocopying, recording, or other electronic or mechanical methods, without the prior written permission of the publisher, except in the case of brief quotations embodied in critical reviews and certain other noncommercial uses permitted by copyright law.

Permissions

For permission requests, please write to the publisher, addressed "Attention: Permissions Coordinator," at the address below:

Test Treasure Publication

Email: support@testtreasure.com

Website: www.testtreasure.com

Unauthorized use or duplication of this material without express and written permission from this site's owner and/or author is strictly prohibited. Excerpts and links may be used, provided that full and clear credit is given to Test Treasure Publication with appropriate and specific direction to the original content.

Trademarks

All trademarks, service marks, and trade names used within this website and Test Treasure Publication's products are proprietary to Test Treasure Publication or other respective owners that have granted Test Treasure Publication the right and license to use such intellectual property.

Disclaimer

While every effort has been made to ensure the accuracy and completeness of the information contained in our products, Test Treasure Publication assumes no responsibility for errors, omissions, or contradictory interpretation of the subject matter herein. All information is provided "as is" without warranty of any kind.

Governing Law

This website is controlled by Test Treasure Publication from our offices located in the state of California, USA. It can be accessed by most countries around the world. As each country has laws that may differ from those of California, by accessing our website, you agree that the statutes and laws of California, without regard to the conflict of laws and the United Nations Convention on the International Sales of Goods, will apply to all matters relating to the use of this website and the purchase of any products or services through this site.

Contents

Introduction	1
Brief Overview of the Exam and Its Importance	4
Detailed Content Review	7
Study Schedules and Planning Advice	10
Frequently Asked Questions	13
1. Language Arts and Reading	16
2. Social Science	28
3. Science	43
4. Mathematics	56
5.1 Full-Length Practice Test 1	69
5.2 Answer Sheet - Practice Test 1	109
6.1 Full-Length Practice Test 2	122
6.2 Answer Sheet - Practice Test 2	161
Test-Taking Strategies	175
Additional Resources	177
Explore Our Range of Study Guides	179

Introduction

Welcome to the "FTCE Elementary Education K-6 Study Guide 2024-2025 Edition," an extraordinary resource meticulously crafted by Test Treasure Publication. We understand the gravity, challenge, and excitement that comes with preparing for the Florida Teacher Certification Examination (FTCE) Elementary Education K-6. The journey ahead is not just about passing an exam; it's about unlocking a fulfilling and impactful career in shaping the minds of tomorrow.

The FTCE Elementary Education K-6 exam is a critical milestone for aspiring teachers in Florida. Success in this examination reflects a profound understanding of subjects that form the foundation of a child's education. Our guide recognizes this and has been designed to be more than just a textbook; it is your mentor and companion throughout your preparation journey.

What's Inside?

This comprehensive guide offers a complete exploration of all core subjects you will encounter in the FTCE Elementary Education K-6 exam:

- **Language Arts and Reading**: From ELA Pedagogy to Literary Analysis and Reading Comprehension.

- **Social Science**: A deep dive into U.S. and World History, Geography, Civics, Economics, and more.

- **Science**: Uncover the principles of Chemistry, Physics, Biology, Geology, and the relationship between Science, Technology, and Society.

- **Mathematics**: Master everything from Rational Numbers and Equations to Probability and Shapes.

Each section is equipped with full-length practice tests, detailed answer explanations, and proven strategies that mirror the actual exam experience.

More Than Just a Study Guide

We go beyond traditional study materials to provide:

- **Detailed Content Review**: Understand every topic thoroughly, leaving no stone unturned.

- **Study Schedules and Planning Advice**: Personalized strategies to organize your preparation.

- **Frequently Asked Questions**: Answers to common questions related to the exam and preparation.

- **Test-Taking Strategies**: Expert tips to enhance your performance.

- **Additional Resources**: Recommended online resources and academic materials to supplement your study.

- **Motivational Insights**: Final words of encouragement to fuel your determination.

A Journey Towards Exceptionalism

At Test Treasure Publication, we believe in cultivating exceptionalism in every learner. Our unwavering commitment to your success shines through in every page of this guide, reflecting our community-driven approach. We invite you to embark on this enriching and uplifting expedition, not just for exam readiness but for a future brimming with boundless opportunities.

Join us on a path illuminated by guidance, support, and the promise of extraordinary success. Your journey begins here.

Brief Overview of the Exam and Its Importance

The Florida Teacher Certification Examination (FTCE) Elementary Education K-6 is a crucial test that holds immense significance for educators aiming to teach in the state of Florida's elementary schools. Administered by the Florida Department of Education, this exam assesses a candidate's knowledge and competence in key subject areas fundamental to elementary education. The following is a concise breakdown of the exam's specifics and its profound importance:

Exam Pattern:

The FTCE Elementary Education K-6 consists of four main subject areas, each with its unique set of questions:

1. **Language Arts and Reading**: 60 questions

2. **Social Science**: 55 questions

3. **Science**: 55 questions

4. **Mathematics**: 60 questions

The test is a computer-based examination comprising a total of 230 multiple-choice questions.

Time:

Candidates are allotted a total of 4 hours and 20 minutes to complete the examination. It is essential to manage time wisely to ensure a thorough review of all questions.

Scoring:

The passing score for the FTCE Elementary Education K-6 is scaled at 200 per subject area. Scores are reported as scaled scores, allowing for a consistent measure of performance across different exam forms.

Importance:

- **Professional Requirement**: The FTCE Elementary Education K-6 exam is a mandatory certification requirement for individuals wishing to teach in Florida's elementary schools (K-6 grades). It verifies the proficiency in essential subjects and pedagogical skills.

- **Quality Assurance**: By assessing educators on core subjects like Language Arts, Mathematics, Science, and Social Science, the examination ensures that teachers possess the knowledge and skills necessary to provide quality education.

- **Career Advancement**: Passing the examination opens doors to various teaching opportunities within Florida, signifying a critical step towards a rewarding teaching career.

- **Reflecting State Standards**: The examination aligns with the Florida state standards for teaching, ensuring that educators are well-prepared to meet the educational needs of their students.

Conclusion:

The FTCE Elementary Education K-6 examination is more than a certification requirement; it symbolizes a commitment to excellence, readiness to inspire young minds, and alignment with the educational values and standards upheld in the state of Florida. Aspiring educators must approach this examination with diligence, understanding its pattern, requirements, and the broader role it plays in shaping the future of education in Florida.

Detailed Content Review

Language Arts and Reading:

ELA Pedagogy: Gain insights into effective teaching methods for English Language Arts, including instructional strategies, assessment techniques, and integrating technology.

Foundations of Grammar: Dive into the fundamental rules of English grammar, including verb tenses, sentence structures, parts of speech, and more.

Literary Analysis: Explore literary devices, genres, themes, and techniques for analyzing literary texts, and build strong reading comprehension skills.

Social Science:

U.S. History: Understand key historical events, periods, and movements that shaped the United States, including Native American history, the Civil War, and the Civil Rights Movement.

World History: Traverse through the major epochs of global history, encompassing ancient civilizations, world wars, and modern global relations.

Geography: Learn about physical and human geography, cartography, and global interconnections, emphasizing geographic literacy.

Economics: Grasp economic principles such as supply and demand, market structures, fiscal policy, and the role of government in economics.

Science:

Scientific Inquiry and Lab Safety: Master the scientific method, experimental design, data analysis, and essential laboratory safety practices.

Chemistry: Explore atomic structure, chemical reactions, periodic trends, and the properties of matter.

Biology: Delve into cellular biology, genetics, evolution, ecology, and the diversity of life.

Physics: Understand principles related to motion, energy, waves, electricity, and magnetism.

Geology: Investigate Earth's structure, rock formation, geological processes, and environmental science.

Mathematics:

Rational Numbers: Build a solid understanding of fractions, decimals, percentages, and their applications.

Equations and Inequalities: Master solving linear equations and inequalities, and explore systems of equations.

Functions: Discover basic and advanced function concepts, including polynomial, exponential, and logarithmic functions.

Probability: Study the principles of probability, statistics, and combinatorics, and their real-world applications.

Two-Dimensional Shapes: Explore geometry concepts such as perimeter, area, angles, and properties of various shapes.

Additional Features:

- **Full-Length Practice Tests**: Simulate the actual exam experience with two practice tests containing 100 questions each.

- **Detailed Answer Explanations**: Understand the reasoning behind each answer with in-depth explanations.

- **Proven Strategies and Tips**: Benefit from expert guidance on time management, question analysis, and effective study methods.

- **Supplementary Resources**: Access recommended online resources and academic materials to enhance your preparation.

Conclusion:

This book's comprehensive coverage ensures that aspiring educators are well-equipped to excel in every aspect of the FTCE Elementary Education K-6 exam. From foundational concepts to advanced topics, from practice tests to personalized guidance, this guide is designed to ignite passion, instill confidence, and lead you to triumph in your academic pursuit.

STUDY SCHEDULES AND PLANNING ADVICE

Preparing for the FTCE Elementary Education K-6 exam is an intensive process that requires careful planning, dedication, and strategic utilization of time. Here, we provide tailored study schedules and planning advice to suit different timelines and individual needs.

1. The 12-Week Study Schedule:

For those who have approximately three months until the exam date, here's a weekly breakdown:

- **Weeks 1-3**: Focus on Language Arts and Reading, diving into ELA Pedagogy, Grammar, and Literary Analysis.

- **Weeks 4-6**: Shift to Social Science, exploring U.S. History, World History, Geography, and Economics.

- **Weeks 7-9**: Delve into Science, covering Chemistry, Physics, Geology, and Biology.

- **Weeks 10-12**: Concentrate on Mathematics, mastering Rational Numbers, Equations, Functions, and Probability.

Tip: Dedicate the final week for comprehensive revision and full-length practice tests.

2. The 8-Week Study Schedule:

If your exam is two months away, consider this accelerated plan:

- **Weeks 1-2**: Focus on Language Arts and Reading.
- **Weeks 3-4**: Explore Social Science topics.
- **Weeks 5-6**: Investigate Science sections.
- **Weeks 7-8**: Dive into Mathematics.

Tip: Integrate review and practice tests throughout the schedule, rather than leaving them to the end.

3. Planning Advice:

- **Set Clear Goals**: Break down the content into manageable daily or weekly objectives. Monitor your progress regularly.
- **Create a Study Environment**: Designate a quiet, organized space for studying, free from distractions.
- **Utilize the Practice Tests**: Regularly assess your understanding using the full-length practice tests in this guide.
- **Stay Healthy**: Remember to maintain a balanced diet, regular exercise, and adequate sleep.
- **Seek Support**: Don't hesitate to seek help from teachers, peers, or online forums if you encounter challenges.
- **Stay Positive and Flexible**: Embrace setbacks as opportunities to learn

and adapt your study plan as needed.

- **Review and Reflect**: Regularly revisit previous topics to reinforce retention.

Conclusion:

The path to success in the FTCE Elementary Education K-6 exam lies in strategic planning, consistent effort, and a positive mindset. Whether you have twelve weeks or eight, these schedules and planning advice are crafted to guide you through a structured and efficient preparation journey.

FREQUENTLY ASKED QUESTIONS

Q1: What is the FTCE Elementary Education K-6 exam, and why is it essential?

A1: The FTCE Elementary Education K-6 exam is a certification test for aspiring educators in Florida's elementary schools. It assesses the candidate's knowledge and competence in subjects essential to elementary education. Passing this exam is a mandatory step towards a teaching career in Florida.

Q2: How is this study guide different from others on the market?

A2: Test Treasure Publishing's study guide offers comprehensive coverage of all exam topics, expert strategies, full-length practice tests, detailed answer explanations, and a community-driven approach. It acts as a mentor, providing personalized learning tailored to individual needs.

Q3: How much time should I devote to studying for the exam?

A3: The ideal study time varies based on individual needs and familiarity with the subjects. Our guide offers both 12-week and 8-week study schedules, allowing you to choose based on your comfort and timeline.

Q4: Are the practice tests in this book similar to the actual exam?

A4: Yes, the practice tests are meticulously designed to mirror the actual exam's format and difficulty, providing an authentic testing experience.

Q5: Can I use this guide if I'm new to some of the subjects covered in the exam?

A5: Absolutely! This guide is crafted to suit learners at different levels, providing foundational knowledge and gradually building up to more advanced concepts.

Q6: Where can I take the FTCE Elementary Education K-6 exam?

A6: The exam is administered by the Florida Department of Education and can be taken at approved testing centers across Florida and some additional locations.

Q7: What if I need further assistance or resources beyond this book?

A7: This study guide includes a section on recommended online resources and academic materials. Additionally, Test Treasure Publishing encourages an open connection with our community, and we're here to support your learning journey.

Q8: How do I know if I'm ready to take the actual exam?

A8: Regular self-assessment using the practice tests and following the structured study schedules will help gauge your readiness. Listen to your confidence level and seek additional support if needed.

Q9: What is Test Treasure Publishing's approach to learning?

A9: Test Treasure Publishing emphasizes personalized learning, mentorship, community-driven engagement, and embracing diversity. Our unwavering dedication to cultivating exceptionalism in every learner sets us apart.

Q10: Where can I purchase this book?

A10: The "FTCE Elementary Education K-6 Study Guide 2024-2025 Edition" is available through major online retailers, including Amazon, and directly through Test Treasure Publishing.

1

LANGUAGE ARTS AND READING

ELA Pedagogy

I gotta say, diving into the world of English Language Arts (ELA) pedagogy is like stepping into a whole new universe. It's like unlocking this secret treasure chest that's filled to the brim with the power of language and literature. And let me tell you, at Test Treasure Publication, we understand that teaching ELA ain't just about boring grammar rules and vocab lists. It's about tapping into kids' imaginations, getting those critical thinking gears turning, and sparking a fiery love for reading and writing.

To really excel in ELA, you gotta take a holistic approach. It's not just about the technical stuff, it's about the artistry and beauty of our language. That's why we've poured our hearts and souls into creating study materials that inspire educators to dive deep into the magic of language and empower their students to become confident communicators.

In the realm of ELA, we cover a whole range of topics. We've got your phonics and spelling, your reading comprehension, and even literary analysis. Our study guide is like a GPS for teachers, guiding them and their students along the winding path to language mastery. We delve into everything from the basics of language acquisition to the nitty-gritty stages of literacy development. Oh, and we've got some killer strategies up our sleeves to promote reading fluency and comprehension.

But let me tell you, one thing we are super passionate about is the power of storytelling. I mean, stories have this crazy ability to transport us to different worlds, make us feel things we've never felt before, and make us question our own beliefs. So, in our study materials, we encourage teachers to embrace the art of storytelling. We want 'em to share captivating stories with their students and guide 'em to create their own masterpieces. We've even got tips on how to choose the perfect stories for each age group, fun reading activities, and ways to foster a classroom vibe that screams "we love literature!"

Now, let's talk about writing. It's a biggie in ELA pedagogy, and we ain't about to let it slide. We know how important it is for students to have killer writing skills. So, our study materials lay out all the strategies a teacher needs to develop those writing muscles. We break down the writing process, give 'em brainstorming techniques, teach 'em how to organize their thoughts, and show 'em how to revise and edit for maximum awesomeness.

But listen, effective ELA pedagogy doesn't stop when the bell rings. We believe in bringing the real world into the classroom. That's why our study materials are all about practical, real-life applications of language skills. We're talking research projects, multimedia presentations, and even those rad collaborative writing ventures. We want students to see that language ain't just something you use in school, but something that's useful and exciting in the real world too.

And let me tell you, as educators dive deep into our study guide, they're gonna be armed with a whole arsenal of instructional strategies, off-the-charts lesson plans, and rockin' assessment tools. By embracing principles like differentiated instruction, teaching that's responsive to different cultures, and multi-modal learning, teachers will be able to meet the needs and learning styles of each and every student. We're all about making sure no one gets left behind in the ELA classroom.

So, welcome to the journey of ELA Pedagogy with Test Treasure Publication! We're here to light that fire inside educators, to unlock the power of language, and to guide students along the path to becoming lifelong learners and lovers of literature. Together, we're gonna create a world where language isn't just a means of communication. It's gonna be a spring of expression, connection, and limitless possibilities. Let's do this!

Foundations of Grammar

Welcome, my fellow language enthusiasts, to a wondrous exploration of the hidden gems nestled within the realm of grammar. Get ready to embark on a journey where we peel back the layers, unraveling the mysteries and complexities that lie within this captivating subject. We're about to dive deep into the heart of grammar, unlocking its power and discovering how it can elevate our writing to new heights.

First things first, let's talk about the building blocks of language—the parts of speech. Nouns, those sturdy pillars that anchor our sentences; verbs, the dynamic engines that breathe life into our writing; adjectives, the vibrant strokes of paint that add color and depth; and adverbs, the graceful dancers that spin around our sentences, adding flair and nuance. Together, they form an exquisite symphony, each playing its unique role, harmonizing with the other components and bringing meaning to our words.

But wait, there's more! We're about to venture beyond the surface and delve into the realm of sentence structure. Picture a beautifully crafted sentence, carefully constructed like a magnificent vehicle to carry our thoughts. But alas, without proper engineering, it can become a chaotic mess. So, hold on tight as we navigate the treacherous waters of subject-verb agreement, sentence fragments, and those sneaky run-on sentences. We'll equip ourselves with the knowledge to build sturdy and coherent prose that captivates our readers.

Now, let's not forget about the unsung heroes of language—punctuation marks. These delightful little creatures have the power to shape the meaning of our words, adding emphasis, pauses, and clarity as needed. From the humble comma, acting as a traffic cop on the page, to the mighty exclamation point, bursting with excitement and emotion, punctuation guides our readers through the twists and turns of our sentences. Get ready to wield these tiny but mighty tools to enhance the impact of our words.

But hold up, grammar is not just a rigid set of rules meant to confine us. It's a living and breathing entity, evolving alongside language itself. So, we shall also embrace the evolving landscape of language usage. From colloquialisms and slang to delightful idioms, these unique expressions bring personality and flavor to our speech and writing. We'll explore the dance between formal and informal language, ensuring we adapt our register to any given situation.

Now, let's roll up our sleeves and get our hands dirty. Through a series of exhilarating exercises, we'll put our newfound knowledge into action. We'll construct sentences like skilled architects, catching any grammatical errors that dare to sneak in. And not only that, we'll scrutinize and analyze different writing styles, honing our skills and refining our command of language. With each exercise conquered, we'll gain confidence to use grammar as a powerful tool for clear and effective communication.

Are you ready to dive into this grammar wonderland, my dear friends? Let us embark on this extraordinary journey, where the beauty of language awaits our discovery. Together, we shall unlock the power of words, enrich our writing, and set sail towards a world of linguistic excellence. Join me as we explore the magical world of grammar—a world where precision and eloquence combine to create masterpieces of expression.

Agreement and Sentence Structure

So here's the thing about grammar, my friend. Agreement is like this magical dance that happens between different parts of a sentence. It's all about getting everything to work together in perfect harmony. We're talking subject-verb agreement, pronoun-antecedent agreement, noun-adjective agreement, and more. It's like a symphony, you know?

Subject-verb agreement is all about that beautiful coordination between the subject and the verb. They've got to be on the same page, in sync, dancing to the same beat. If you've got a singular subject, you need a singular verb. And if you've got a whole gang of plural subjects, well, you better bring out the plural verb. That way, there's no awkward mismatch messing up the rhythm.

Then we've got pronoun-antecedent agreement, which is like adding another layer of harmony to our sentences. Those little pronouns, like "he," "she," and "it," have to match up with their antecedents. Same number, same person, same gender. It's like they're playing dress-up and trying to blend in with their antecedents, without causing any confusion or mix-ups.

And let's not forget about noun-adjective agreement. This is where adjectives become loyal sidekicks to our nouns. They've got to mirror the number and gender of the nouns they're describing. It's all about creating this seamless connection, so that when people read or hear the words, they can see it all in their minds like a vivid picture.

But here's the thing, my friend. It's not just about agreement. The way we put our sentences together is crucial too. It's like building a house. You start with a strong foundation, a captivating opening that grabs attention and sets the stage for what's to come. It's like the welcome mat, inviting people in for the ride.

Then comes the meat of the message, the middle section of the sentence. This is where we develop our ideas, make our arguments, and really let our emotions shine. It's all about finding the right structure, using transitions to guide the reader through and keeping things organized and logical. That way, everyone can follow along and really get what we're saying.

And finally, we wrap it all up with a satisfying ending. This is where we leave a lasting impression, my friend. Maybe we offer a reflection that makes folks stop and think. Or maybe we make a bold statement that sticks with them long after they've read the words. It's about leaving our mark, you know?

But here's the thing, my friend. Mastering agreement and sentence structure isn't just about following a bunch of rules. It's an art form. It's about taking our communication to new levels, giving our words power and clarity. It's like magic, really. With practice and understanding, we can craft sentences that captivate, inspire, and connect with others.

So let's dive into the details of agreement and sentence structure, my friend. Let's unravel the mysteries and discover the hidden gems that lie within. Together, we'll embark on a journey of discovery and mastery, honing our skills and crafting sentences that make a lasting impression on all who come across them. Are you ready? Let's do this.

Punctuation

Welcome, my friend, to this captivating section of our study guide. Here, we embark on a thrilling journey into the fascinating world of punctuation. Get ready to unravel its secrets and unlock its immense potential - it's going to be quite the adventure!

Punctuation, my friend, is no ordinary collection of random marks on a page. Oh no, it's the very foundation of clarity and structure. Let's start our exploration with the unassuming, yet mighty, comma. This humble hero brings harmony to sentences, allowing ideas to breathe and find their rightful place. Through vivid examples and meticulous explanations, we'll dive into the art of using commas to separate elements, create lists, and add emphasis.

Now, let's shift our focus to two trusty sidekicks - the period and the question mark. These steadfast sentinels signify the end of a thought or awaken our curiosity. We'll uncover the subtle differences in their usage, mastering the delicate balance between making a statement and sparking a question. Through practice exercises and quizzes, we'll build your confidence in punctuating sentences with precision, and leaving your readers hanging on your every word.

Alright, dear friend, time to level up. We're venturing into the world of semicolons and colons. These often misunderstood punctuation marks bridge the gaps between ideas, infusing authority and order. With our expert guidance, you'll unravel the intricacies of combining clauses, organizing information, and forging meaningful connections. Your writing will undergo a transformative metamorphosis, exuding sophistication and commanding attention.

But wait, there's more! We can't forget about dashes and parentheses. Ah, the allure of these enchanting yet mysterious punctuation marks. They bring drama and intimacy to your words, allowing you to highlight digressions, provide clarifications, and stir emotions. Get ready to create a tapestry of meaning that captures the hearts and minds of your readers.

Throughout this journey, my dear companion, we'll be by your side. We'll guide you through the labyrinth of punctuation rules, providing you with the essential tools to master this subtle art. Our practice exercises and comprehensive explanations will not only help you understand the theoretical underpinnings but also develop the practical skills to punctuate with precision and grace.

So, my friend, I invite you to join us on this enchanting adventure through the realm of punctuation. Together, we'll transform the power of mere marks on a page into a symphony of clarity and expression. Let Test Treasure Publication be your guiding light, propelling you towards mastery and illuminating the path to extraordinary success in the realm of the written word. Are you ready? Let's go!

Vocabulary and Word Relationships

Listen, my friend, let's get real for a moment. Here at Test Treasure Publication, we get how crucial vocab is for nailing your academic game. It's not just about sounding fancy, it's about really understanding and connecting with what you're learning. We've got your back when it comes to mastering words and using them like a pro.

You see, words aren't just random letters put together. They have relationships with each other. It's like a big web of meanings and contexts. And if you wanna navigate this crazy language world, you need to know the ins and outs of these word relationships.

So, let's start with synonyms and antonyms. Synonyms are like different flavors of the same ice cream, ya know? They're words that kinda mean the same thing but give you options to spice up your sentences. Mastering synonyms means you'll have a whole arsenal of words to express yourself in a fancy way.

Now, antonyms are the opposite. They're like salt and sugar, complete opposites that make your taste buds go wild. Understanding antonyms not only makes you sound smarter, but it also helps you pick up on the subtle differences in meaning. Trust me, it's like a secret weapon for diving deep into words.

But hold on, my friend, we're not done. Next up, we've got homophones. These sneaky words sound the same but mean totally different things. Ain't that just something? We've got some tricks up our sleeves to help you sort through the confusion and choose the right word every time.

Now, let's dive into the world of word families and derivations. It's like a whole ecosystem of words, you know? Word families are like a group of siblings, each with their own unique traits but connected through a common background. Understanding how all these words relate to each other will make your vocab game skyrocket.

And derivations? Well, that's like creating new words using bits and pieces. It's like playing mad scientist with language. By digging into where words come from, you can easily crack the code of unfamiliar words and impress everyone with your wizardry.

Last but not least, we're gonna talk about context clues. Picture this: you're reading a passage and stumble upon a tricky word you don't know. But fear not, my friend, because within those very words, there are hidden hints and clues that will help you unravel its mysterious meaning. We'll teach you how to read between the lines and become a pro word detective.

Alright, my friend, we've poured all our blood, sweat, and tears into creating study materials that will revolutionize your vocab game. We've got interactive exercises, mind-blowing examples, and explanations that break down even the trickiest of language puzzles. We're here to make language your superpower.

So, join us on this epic journey of enlightening discoveries. We'll equip you with the tools and knowledge to conquer the wild world of vocab and word relationships. Consider us your trusty sidekick as you navigate this crazy language universe and kick butt in the FTCE Elementary Education K-6 exam. And hey, the sky's the limit, my friend. Let's do this!

Literary Analysis

Alright, folks, buckle up because we're about to dive into the exhilarating world of literary analysis. It's not just about breaking down a boring old piece of writing, no way. It's a skill that lets us unravel all the hidden meanings and emotions that are woven into the very fabric of a text. Authors are like master weavers, using subtle nuances, symbolism, and jaw-dropping imagery to create these mind-blowing works of art that just beg us to jump right in.

In this chapter, we're gonna take a deep dive into understanding and interpreting all those fancy literary devices. We'll start by unraveling the twists and turns of plot development – you know, all the juicy stuff that keeps us on the edge of our seats. We've got exposition, rising action, climax, falling action, and resolution. Trust me, it's like getting caught in a wild roller coaster ride, filled with tension and release, and by the end, you'll be in awe of how these authors manage to capture our hearts and minds.

Next up, we're gonna get up close and personal with these literary characters. It's like peeking into their souls and figuring out what makes 'em tick. We'll analyze their actions, their motivations, and the flaws that make 'em oh-so-real. It's like taking a magnifying glass to their lives, decoding their deepest thoughts and desires, and uncovering all the messy details of their epic journeys.

Now, let's enter the enchanted realm of themes and symbolism – where imagination and deeper meanings go hand in hand. Here's where things really start to get interesting. We'll unveil all those hidden messages, moral lessons, and sneaky allegorical references that make a text come alive. Trust me, there's a whole universe of symbols waiting to be deciphered. Even the most innocent objects or settings hold crazy amounts of meaning, and it's up to us cool kids to reveal their secrets.

But hold on tight 'cause we can't overlook the power of language and style. We're gonna dig deep into words, sentences, and all that fancy figurative language. Yeah, we're talking metaphors, similes, personification, and more. It's like unwrapping pretty little presents one by one, each with its own unique emotions, depth, and artistry.

And finally, we're gonna go full-on critical analysis mode. We'll sharpen our critical thinking skills and dig into literature within historical, societal, and cultural contexts. We're gonna have some serious discussions, exploring how literature impacts society and how society shapes literature. It's gonna open our eyes to a whole new way of seeing things – we'll realize that literature isn't just about entertainment, it's a force that can change the world and enlighten our souls.

So my literary adventurers, are you ready for this amazing journey into the depths of literary analysis? Are you ready to set sail, armed with the tools of awesomeness, and unlock the secrets of timeless classics and mind-bending contemporary works? Well then, let's go, my friends. Together, we're gonna unlock the magic within the pages of books and unleash our own creative spirits.

Reading Comprehension

Let's dive into the wild world of reading comprehension, my friend. It's more than just figuring out what the heck the words on a page mean. Nah, reading comprehension is an art form. It's about taking a text and understanding not just the literal words, but the deeper message. It's like deciphering a secret code, unraveling the author's intentions, and weaving in your own knowledge and experiences. It ain't no simple task, I tell ya. It requires you to jump in headfirst and really think critically.

Now, within the realm of reading comprehension, there are all sorts of elements you gotta wrap your head around. One of 'em is textual analysis. It's like being a detective, digging into the structure of a text - the way it's organized, the tone, and even the point of view. This kind of stuff helps you get to the heart of what the author is trying to say.

But wait, there's more! You gotta have the superpower of inference to truly rock at reading comprehension. Inference is all about reading between the lines, picking up on clues and evidence scattered throughout the text. It's like being a mindreader, ferreting out the hidden meanings and subtle nuances that lie beneath the surface.

And don't get me started on main ideas and supporting details. These bad boys are like the lighthouse in a storm, guiding you through the choppy seas of a text. The main idea is the anchor point, the big picture that everything else in the text revolves around. It's like finding the piece of the puzzle that makes everything else make sense.

But hey, we can't forget about the power of words themselves. The words we come across in a text can pack a real punch, my friend. Understanding the context they're used in is like turning on a light bulb - it helps us see the tone, purpose, and even the implications of the text in a whole new way.

As you embark on this crazy reading comprehension journey, it's important to develop some killer strategies. Like predicting and previewing - using what you already know to make educated guesses about what's coming up. And active reading techniques, like highlighting, making notes, and summarizing, to keep yourself engaged and make sure you're really taking in the important stuff.

Here at Test Treasure Publication, we live and breathe this stuff. We're all about delivering study materials that will blow your mind and transform your reading abilities. Our study guide for the FTCE Elementary Education K-6 exam is the ultimate key to unlocking your full potential. So come join us on this incredible journey, my friend. We're gonna light up the path to success and open the doors to a future filled with endless possibilities. Let's do this!

2

SOCIAL SCIENCE

U.S. History

Come on in, folks, and step into the realm of Test Treasure Publication's U.S. History study guide! It's like cracking open a time capsule, where the past comes alive, painting a vivid picture of the American story. Get ready to be fully immersed as we embark on a mind-blowing journey through the ages, diving deep into the very foundations that shaped this great nation.

We've got everything covered here - from the Native American civilizations that flourished long before those Europeans showed up, to the epic struggles and triumphant moments of the American Revolution. This study guide doesn't leave a single stone unturned, folks! We're taking you on a rollercoaster ride, showcasing the incredible feats of visionaries like George Washington, Benjamin Franklin, and Thomas Jefferson, who fearlessly paved the way towards independence and self-governance.

And hold on tight, because we're just getting started! As we navigate through the vast expanse of history, get ready to explore the incredible hardships endured by brave men and women who fought tooth and nail for the abolition of slavery during the Civil War. We're talking about folks like Abraham Lincoln, Frederick Douglass, and Harriet Tubman - the real heroes who pushed for a more inclusive and just society.

Now, folks, within the pages of our study guide, we're shining a light on the voices of the suffragettes, those badass warriors who fought relentlessly for women's rights. And let's not forget about the transformative era of the Industrial Revolution, where things were shifting and shaking like nobody's business. We're delving into the untold stories of immigrants who came over to these American shores, folks who shaped the very fabric of our great nation.

But we're not stopping there, folks! Get ready to dive into the trenches of World War I, the heartbreak of the Great Depression, and the sheer madness of World War II. These events shook the nation and the world, and we're giving you a front-row seat to witness it all. You'll see that the American spirit, in the face of war, always comes out stronger and more united.

And let me tell you, folks, we don't shy away from the important stuff. We're exploring the civil rights movement like nobody's business - a time when the voices of incredible leaders like Dr. Martin Luther King Jr., Rosa Parks, and Malcolm X rang out loud and clear. This pivotal period in history was defined by the fight for equality and justice, a fight that echoed across the nation.

But wait, there's more! Our U.S. History study guide goes beyond the dates and facts, folks. We're diving into the intricate nuances and societal shifts that have shaped our very American identity. We'll unpack the impact of landmark Supreme Court cases like Brown v. Board of Education and Roe v. Wade, moments that forever changed the course of history.

And don't think we're done just yet! We're immersing ourselves in the dynamic narratives of the Cold War, the Space Race, and the whirlwind changes of the modern era. We're digging deep into contemporary events like the 9/11 attacks and the election of the first African American president, because we need to understand the complexities of our rapidly evolving world.

So here's the deal, folks: By journeying through our U.S. History study guide, you're not just going to unlock the secrets of the past - you're going to awaken the historian within. We're going to ignite a passion for the past and empower you with a comprehensive understanding of the events and figures that have shaped the nation we know today. Welcome to Test Treasure Publication, where together, we're going to light up the path to extraordinary success!

World History

But first, let's paint the scene, shall we? I want you to imagine with me for a moment. Picture yourself standing at the edge of a crumbling ancient civilization, peering into the vast expanse of time. Can you see it? Good. Now, visualize the magnificent pyramids of Egypt, defying gravity and standing tall as a testament to human ingenuity. Imagine the awe-inspiring Roman Empire, flexing its muscles and conquering vast lands that left an indelible mark on the world. And don't forget the richness of Chinese dynasties, their culture injecting life into the veins of history even to this day.

World History isn't just a stuffy old subject – it's a gateway to understanding the tapestry of human existence. It invites us to step outside ourselves, to witness the triumphs and tribulations of long-gone civilizations. It's like a time machine, transporting us to witness the rise and fall of empires, the intricate dance of cultures, and the mighty display of ideas.

In this study guide, we're going places, my friend. Together, we'll wander the globe, diving headfirst into the pivotal moments and extraordinary figures that have shaped World History. Brace yourself, because we're unearthing the secrets of ancient civilizations, from the fertile banks of the Nile to the bustling streets of ancient Athens. We'll witness the birth and growth of great empires, from the awe-inspiring Mongol Empire to the iron grip of the British Empire. And get ready, because we're diving headfirst into the turbulent events of the modern era, from the heart-wrenching horrors of World War II to the inspiring victories of social movements.

But wait! This journey isn't just about memorizing cold, hard facts. No, no. We go deeper than that in the hallowed halls of Test Treasure Publication. We're about breathing life into the history books, peeling back the layers to reveal the juicy stories hidden within. We believe that history isn't just a bunch of events listed on a timeline – it's a vivid tapestry woven from human experiences, emotions, and dreams. So get ready to meet the heroes and villains, witness the moments that changed the course of history, and feel the triumphs and heartaches that still echo within us today.

Come on! Join us on this grand adventure, dear reader. Together, we'll voyage through time, guided by our insatiable hunger for knowledge and the thrill of discovery. We'll uncover the mysteries of the past, illuminating the path to a deeper understanding of our world. Within the pages of this study guide lies a treasure trove of historical insights, waiting for you to embrace the extraordinary in your quest for knowledge. Welcome to Test Treasure Publication, where we breathe life into the past and the world is yours to explore.

Social Studies Skills and Pedagogy

Step 1: Understanding the Scope of Social Studies

Hey there! So, when we talk about social studies, we're not just talking about memorizing dates and facts, my friend. It's way bigger than that. It's like diving deep into the ocean of humanity, exploring different civilizations, and trying to make sense of the world we live in. We're talking about culture, geography, history, economics, and even government. It's a whole adventure!

Step 2: Nurturing Inquiry and Critical Thinking

Here at Test Treasure Publication, we know that curiosity is where it's at, my friend. We believe that social studies is all about exploring, asking questions, and thinking critically. That's why we've carefully crafted study materials that'll ignite that fire within you, making you wonder about everything around you and pushing you to dig deeper for those answers. By honing these skills, we want you to be in the driver's seat of your own learning journey.

Step 3: Integrating Multiple Perspectives

In a world that's so connected, it's super important to understand and appreciate different points of view, right? That's where social studies comes in, my friend. It gives you a chance to explore diverse cultures, histories, and ways of thinking. Our study guides don't just give you the full picture, but they also teach you the value of understanding and respecting other people's viewpoints. We want you to be part of meaningful discussions, debates, and analysis so that you can broaden your horizons and develop that global mindset.

Step 4: Developing Historical Literacy

History is like the secret sauce of social studies, my friend. You see, by understanding the past, we get a solid foundation to understand the present and shape the future. At Test Treasure Publication, we know how important it is for you to be a history buff and understand how social, political, and economic systems work. That's why our study materials take you through the stories of time, highlighting major events, important people, and significant movements. We want you to feel the pulse of the past and appreciate the rollercoaster ride of the human experience.

Step 5: Utilizing Primary and Secondary Sources

To really get a grip on social studies, my friend, you can't just rely on those boring textbooks. Nope! You gotta dive headfirst into primary and secondary sources. We'll teach you how to analyze and evaluate all sorts of cool stuff like letters, speeches, photographs, maps, and diaries. By getting hands-on with these authentic sources, you'll sharpen your analytical skills, understand things from different perspectives, and really grasp the complexities of history.

Step 6: Incorporating Technology

Okay, let's be real here. We're living in the digital age, and technology is where it's at, my friend. And we're all about blending the old with the new. At Test Treasure Publication, we're not afraid to use technology to enhance your social studies journey. Our study materials are loaded with interactive multimedia, online resources, and virtual simulations that'll take you on a wild ride of learning. By fusing traditional teaching methods with cutting-edge technology, we're making sure you're ready for the future and equipped with essential digital skills.

Step 7: Engaging in Active Citizenship

Guess what, my friend? Social studies isn't just confined to the four walls of the classroom. It's about empowering you to be an active citizen and a force for change in our awesome democratic society. We strongly believe in nurturing your civic responsibility and igniting that fire within you for social justice. Our study guides don't just teach you about political systems – they inspire you to have critical conversations, stand up for what you believe in, and get involved in your community. We want you to be informed, take action, and be the change you wanna see in the world.

Step 8: Assessment and Reflection

Hey, we all gotta know where we're at, right? That's why assessment is so important. At Test Treasure Publication, we've got you covered. Our assessment tools cover all the bases, from multiple-choice questions to essays, projects, and performance-based tasks. But it's not just about testing what you know. We want you to think critically, apply those skills we've built together, and reflect on your own growth as a learner. Through self-reflection and feedback, you'll own your learning journey and keep improving.

Embark on the Journey

So my friend, Test Treasure Publication is where it's at when it comes to Social Studies Skills and Pedagogy. We're here to take you on an adventure like no other. Together, we'll dive into the depths of social studies, ignite that passion within you, and equip you with the skills to rock it academically. You're not just gonna be a bystander – you'll be an active participant in shaping our world. So come on, join us on this extraordinary journey at Test Treasure Publication. Trust us, something amazing is waiting for you!

Geography

Have you ever wondered about the incredible secrets our Earth holds? Well, the study of geography is like a key that opens up a window, giving us a glimpse into the amazing physical features, climate patterns, and the intricate connection between humans and our environment. It's like exploring a world full of wonders, from the majestic Himalayas to the vast expanse of the Amazon rainforest. Picture it, the Earth is like a mesmerizing tapestry overflowing with natural beauty.

But geography isn't just about landforms, it's about understanding how we humans interact with our surroundings too. By figuring out where people live, how they move, and the impact they have on the environment, we get a deeper understanding of the complex web of relationships that shape our societies. And let me tell you, it's not always a walk in the park.

When we study geography, we're equipped with the tools to unravel the mysteries behind our planet's landscapes and ecosystems. We can analyze how climate change is affecting vulnerable regions, study the causes and consequences of natural disasters, and even come up with strategies to lessen their impact. And that's not all, geography also helps us make sense of the crazy interconnectedness of our globalized world. This web of economic, political, and social interactions shapes the way we live today.

Want to know something mind-blowing? Let's look at the mind-boggling disparities in wealth and development between different regions around the world. We can see how natural resources play a role in shaping economies, and how the forces of globalization impact indigenous communities. And let's not forget about the unequal distribution of power and resources that keeps the world spinning.

So, as we dive into this study guide together, get ready to embark on a thrilling exploration. We'll dissect maps, analyze spatial relationships, and learn about the incredible cultures and environmental challenges scattered across the globe. Geography is all about fueling your curiosity and broadening your horizons.

At Test Treasure Publication, we're on a mission to provide you with an immersive study experience like no other. Our study materials are carefully crafted to help you understand the fascinating intricacies of our world. So, as you flip through the pages of this guide, let the rivers, mountains, and cities become familiar landmarks on your journey to success. We're here to guide you every step of the way.

Join us on this enlightening journey where geography becomes more than just an ordinary study. Get ready to discover the extraordinary wonders of our planet and embrace the power of knowledge. Together, let's navigate the terrain of geography, igniting a passion for exploration and a deep appreciation for the incredible interconnectedness of our world.

U.S. Government

Welcome to this chapter of our study guide! We're about to uncover the foundational principles that lay the groundwork for our government. It's like exploring a maze of corridors, where we'll uncover the secrets that keep our political structure in a delicate balance.

But before we dive into the nitty-gritty, let's take a moment to reflect on the birth of our nation. It's a captivating story of revolution, independence, and the relentless pursuit of freedom. Our United States is built on ideals and values that still shine brightly today. The Declaration of Independence and the Constitution are the blueprints of our democracy, crafted by visionary leaders that we owe a debt of gratitude.

Now, let's dig deeper into the three branches of government: the executive, legislative, and judicial branches. With a fine-tooth comb, we'll uncover their roles, responsibilities, and powers, revealing the complex tapestry of governance. We'll explore everything from what the President does to how laws are made in Congress. This will give you a comprehensive understanding of how our nation makes decisions.

But hold on, we can't forget about federalism! It's the cornerstone of our government structure. It's all about the balance of power between the federal government and the states, walking a tightrope between central authority and regional autonomy. It's a delicate dance that shows the very foundation our nation is built upon.

Oh, and of course, let's not overlook the electoral process! It's the heartbeat of democracy. From the thrilling primary elections to the mind-boggling Electoral College, we'll unlock the secrets of how our country elects its leadership. By the time we're done, you'll have all the tools you need to engage in the democratic process as an informed and active citizen.

As we wrap up our journey through the world of U.S. Government, take a moment to reflect on the immense responsibility that comes with understanding our governance. This isn't just about acing your exam, it's about recognizing and appreciating the democratic values that shape our nation. Each page turned and concept understood brings you one step closer to being an empowered citizen, ready to make a meaningful contribution to our government and society.

So join us on this transformative journey! Together, we'll unlock a treasure trove of knowledge and understanding, empowering you to navigate the corridors of governance and shape the future of our nation. It's more than just learning—it's an adventure!

Civics and Citizenship

As we dive into the realm of Civics and Citizenship, get ready to embark on an exhilarating journey into the depths of our nation's history. It's not just some boring study of dates and events, but a profound exploration of what really defines our great nation - the very essence of democracy. From the epic birth of the United States to the modern-day challenges we face, this chapter is going to shine a light on our civic responsibilities and show us the sheer power of being an active citizen.

So, let's start our historical timeline in 1776, when our country was born with a loud bang - the signing of the Declaration of Independence. Those brave souls boldly declared our desire for independence from the clutches of colonial rule. Their words created the foundation for this incredible nation we call home. They etched the principles of liberty, equality, and justice for all deep into the fabric of our being, and those principles have echoed through the ages, shaping everything that makes America, America.

Moving forward, the next big milestone on our timeline is the Constitutional Convention of 1787. It was there that our founding fathers, those brilliant minds, meticulously crafted the framework for our government. They brought the United States Constitution to life, which became the ultimate guide, ensuring our individual freedoms, the separation of powers, and a system of checks and balances. This was the moment that solidified our governance system and showed just how intelligent those framers really were.

As we venture further along this historical timeline, we're going to encounter some pivotal events that shook our society to its core and pushed our democratic principles to the limit. The abolitionist movement and the Civil War were no joke. The Emancipation Proclamation, issued by President Abraham Lincoln in 1863, was a game-changer that turned the tide against slavery and sparked a battle for civil rights that rages on to this very day. These struggles are a constant reminder that no matter what, citizens have the power to bring about change through collective action.

Fast forward to the 20th century, and we hit some pretty major milestones. The women's suffrage movement fought tooth and nail until the Nineteenth Amendment was ratified in 1920, finally granting women the right to vote. It was a powerful moment, a testament to the strength of grassroots movements and the relentless efforts of courageous individuals who fought fervently for equal representation.

Then comes the Civil Rights Movement of the 50s and 60s. This period is monumental in our timeline as it showcases the unwavering determination of brave activists fighting for equal rights for all Americans. From the Montgomery Bus Boycott to the iconic March on Washington, these incredible people stood up against racial discrimination, and their efforts resulted in groundbreaking legislation like the Civil Rights Act of 1964 and the Voting Rights Act of 1965. These victories should always remind us that each and every citizen has the potential to make an everlasting impact on society.

Now we're almost caught up to the present day, where our historical timeline meets contemporary challenges and opportunities. We witness the rise of social activism and grassroots movements tackling important issues such as climate change, income inequality, and police reform. And let me tell you, these movements embody the true spirit of active citizenship. They're out there, holding our government accountable and making sure the principles our nation was built on continue to shine in every generation.

As we venture further into this journey of Civics and Citizenship, we're not only going to learn about the past, but we'll also realize just how important our roles as responsible citizens are in shaping the future. We'll understand that participating in the democratic process isn't just a suggestion - it's a must. It's through our knowledge, our understanding, our empathy, and our action that we can honor the vision of our founding fathers and propel our nation towards a future that's inclusive and just.

So, are you ready to dive into the annals of American history with me? Let's unravel the rich tapestry of our nation's past, uncover the triumphs and challenges that molded our society, and embrace that fiery spirit of civic engagement that beats at the heart of our democratic heritage. Together, let's pave the way for a brighter future, one built on those cherished principles of liberty, justice, and the indomitable spirit of the American people. Let the adventure begin!

Economics

Chapter 1: Introduction to Economics

Alright, folks, welcome to the wild world of economics! In this first chapter, we're gonna dive deep into the fundamental concepts that make this field tick. We're talking about the crazy balance between scarcity and our never-ending wants. Can you believe it? The struggle to get what we want is real!

But wait, there's more! We'll also uncover the secrets of supply and demand and how they control the prices of stuff in the marketplace. And trust me, we won't bore you with just theories and equations. We'll bring in real-life examples and captivating case studies that will paint a picture so vivid, you'll feel like you're right in the middle of all these economic decisions and forces that shape our consumer-driven society.

Chapter 2: Macroeconomics

Alright, time to zoom out a bit and take a look at the big picture. Macroeconomics is all about analyzing the entire economy of a country or even the whole world. We're not just talking about your everyday transactions here, we're looking at the health and stability of a whole nation's economy.

We'll dive into some macroeconomic indicators like GDP, inflation, and unemployment. These indicators give us insights into how well or not-so-well an economy is doing. But we won't stop there! We'll also dig into the impact of government policies, fiscal and monetary measures, and even international trade on a nation's overall economic well-being. Trust me, the bigger the economy, the crazier it gets!

Chapter 3: Microeconomics

Alright, time to focus our lens on the individual markets. Microeconomics lets us dig deep into the behavior of consumers and firms, uncovering what makes them tick. We wanna know what factors drive their decisions, what makes them want to buy or sell. It's like peeking behind the scenes of the economic world.

We'll explore concepts like elasticities, market structures, and the costs involved. But don't worry, we won't leave you hanging with just theories. We'll bring in case studies and real-world examples that will show you exactly how these microeconomic principles play out in different sectors. Think agriculture, technology, anything and everything! You'll be armed with the knowledge to make informed decisions in your own life and career.

Chapter 4: International Economics

Now, here comes the big one - international economics. In this chapter, we're gonna unravel the mysteries of globalization. We'll explore how goods, services, and ideas flow between countries like there's no tomorrow. It's like watching a massive puzzle come together!

We'll dive into concepts like comparative advantage, exchange rates, and trade policies. Sounds fancy, right? Well, we'll break it down in a way that will make you say, "Oh, I get it now!". Real-world examples will show you how global economic interdependence can impact local economies. It's like a chain reaction, folks. Seeing how nations are connected in the modern world will blow your mind!

Chapter 5: Economic Systems

Alright, last but definitely not least, we're gonna talk about economic systems. Every society operates within a certain economic system, and in this chapter, we're gonna explore them all. We've got market economies, command economies, and even mixed economies in the mix. Each of them has their own strengths and weaknesses, kinda like choosing between that perfect pair of shoes or that juicy burger.

But here's the cool part - by understanding the principles behind these economic models, you'll be able to critically evaluate them. You'll have the power to see how they impact society in different ways. We're gonna have lively debates and analytical discussions that will really make you think. It's all about understanding the advantages and challenges associated with different economic systems, my friends.

Conclusion: A World of Possibilities

Alright, folks, we've reached the end of this epic journey through the realm of economics. But don't worry, the adventure doesn't stop here! Take a moment to reflect on all the knowledge and insights you've gained along the way. Economics isn't just about numbers and graphs, it's about understanding our complex global society. You've got the power to make informed decisions, actively participate in the economy, and contribute to a better society.

So hold on tight, because with Test Treasure Publication as your guide, get ready to uncover the wonders, challenges, and infinite possibilities of the world of economics. It's gonna light up your path and empower you to navigate the crazy world of the global economy. Get ready for the ride of your life!

3

SCIENCE

Scientific Inquiry and Lab Safety

Step 1: Understanding Scientific Inquiry

Alright, folks, strap in because we're about to dive headfirst into the fascinating world of scientific inquiry. This ain't just some ordinary process, it's an art that opens the doors to endless exploration. Scientific inquiry is driven by our insatiable curiosity, our desire for knowledge, and our never-ending quest for answers. So, get ready to awaken your inner scientist as we question, hypothesize, investigate, and draw conclusions. Our study guide is like a magical journey that will take you through the ins and outs of the scientific method, giving you real-life examples that will ignite your imagination and leave you thirsting for more.

Step 2: Embracing the Laboratory

Now, picture this: we're stepping into the sacred haven of the laboratory, where theories are put to the test and ideas come to life. But hold up! We can't just waltz in there all willy-nilly. Safety first, my friends! The lab is a place that demands utmost respect and adherence to safety protocols. Why, you ask? Well, that's because we want you to not only protect yourselves but also create an environment where learning can flourish without any danger lurking around. Our study materials have got your back, meticulously outlining all the lab safety procedures you need to know - from proper attire to handling hazardous materials. We're all about fostering a culture of safety and responsibility, so we'll provide you with practical tips, vivid illustrations, and engaging scenarios that'll empower you to create a safe and enriching laboratory experience.

Step 3: Hands-on Exploration

Now, teachers, listen up! Your role goes beyond just spouting out theories and concepts. We want you to give your students the chance to get their hands dirty and truly experience science. Our study guide is chock-full of exciting inquiry-based experiments specially designed for elementary school kids. We're talking about everything from simple chemical reactions to the wonderful mysteries of nature. Each experiment is carefully thought out to spark curiosity and ignite critical thinking. Not only that, but we also provide you with detailed instructions, safety precautions, and thought-provoking questions. Get ready to bring the magic of science to life in your own classroom!

Step 4: Reflection and Growth

Listen, people, it's not just about cramming your brain with facts and figures. We believe that true growth comes from looking back at your experiences, analyzing the ups and downs of your scientific journey, and figuring out how you can become an even better teacher. Our study guide is all about encouraging you to reflect and become self-aware. We're here to fire up your introspective engine with thought-provoking questions and open-ended discussions. Get ready to embark on your own personal growth journey and emerge as a more effective and inspiring educator.

Step 5: Community Engagement

Alright, let's talk about the power of unity, my friends. We're all about building a strong community that fosters a love for science and collective growth. Through our study guide, we want you to connect with other passionate educators, aspiring scientists, and scientific organizations. We've got suggestions for professional development opportunities, online discussion forums, and interactive platforms where you can collaborate, exchange ideas, and expand your understanding of scientific inquiry and lab safety. Together, we'll create a network of science enthusiasts who are ready to take on the world.

Embarking on this chapter of Scientific Inquiry and Lab Safety is like going on an epic adventure. It's a thrilling exploration that will shape you as a teacher and inspire your young learners. At Test Treasure Publication, we're right by your side every step of the way, shining a light on the path to extraordinary success. So, let's join forces and embark on this transformative journey together. Science isn't just some boring subject; it's a lifelong passion, a gateway to a future overflowing with knowledge and wonder. Get ready, my friends, because this is where ordinary learning takes a leap into the extraordinary.

Science, Technology, and Society

Hey there! Welcome to the mind-blowing world of Science, Technology, and Society. Get ready to dive into the crazy connections between these three game-changers and see how they shape the world we live in. It's like this ol' dance where they all rely on each other to create something amazing.

First thing's first, science is all about being super curious. It's like a detective trying to unlock the secrets of the natural world by studying, experimenting, and analyzing everything it can get its hands on. And guess what? That leads to all these badass technological advancements that push us humans to do things we never thought possible. And that, my friend, is what changes society in a big way.

So, buckle up for a trip through time as we look at the incredible tech marvels that have blown our minds. We're talkin' about stuff like the wheel, the printing press, the steam engine, and all the way up to the Internet, smartphones, and even artificial intelligence. Each one of these innovations has totally rocked our world, transforming how we communicate, learn, work, and hang out.

But it's not just technology calling the shots here. Society is a major player in this dance too. It both drives and is shaped by science and technology. Society's needs, desires, and dreams drive scientific progress, giving researchers the motivation to try new things. And at the same time, scientific breakthroughs and new gadgets shape society, changing how we think, behave, and live our lives.

Now, let's talk ethics, my friend. In the midst of all this progress, we've got to think about the consequences. We can't just go wild with all these awesome advancements without considering how they might affect people, communities, and the environment. So, buckle up for some deep discussions on topics like bioethics, privacy, and sustainability. It's all about finding that balance between progress and the well-being of everyone.

Speaking of responsibility, it's up to all of us to think about the ethical side of things. By keeping our eye on the greater good and looking out for the well-being of humanity and the world we live in, we can make sure that progress has a positive impact.

Okay, we're almost done, but don't worry, the excitement's not over yet. We're standing on the edge of a crazy future filled with even more mind-blowing discoveries and innovations. We're talking about stuff that's gonna make our jaws drop, my friend. Imagine a world where science and technology work together perfectly, while still keeping us humans happy and thriving.

So, join us on this wild journey through the world of Science, Technology, and Society. We'll learn so much together and ignite that fire in our bellies for these awesome forces of change. By embracing these ideas, we'll open doors to endless opportunities, never-ending progress, and a society that's all about knowledge, compassion, and working together.

Hey, you're not alone in this, though. Test Treasure Publication is here to guide and empower you along the way. Get ready to unlock the secrets to extraordinary success and become the catalysts for a brighter, more enlightened world. Let's do this!

Chemistry

Join me on a wild ride through time, my friend, as we trace the footsteps of the fearless pioneers who turned chemistry into the mind-blowing field it is today. Our journey starts back in the ancient days, when the very foundations of chemical knowledge were being laid.

Picture this: it's 3000 BCE, and in ancient Mesopotamia, those clever folks were churning out clay tablets that held the secrets to brewing beer and baking bread. Little did they know, they were starting a revolution of chemical transformations. As time moved on, these ancient civilizations dabbled in the realm of colors, using natural materials to create vibrant dyes that made their temples and tombs pop.

Now, let's fast forward to ancient Greece, the holy grail of Western civilization. Thinkers like Democritus were dropping bombshells left and right with their theories about little things called atoms - the tiny building blocks of matter. Then we had the smashing Aristotle, who was busy trying to unravel the deep connections between all the elements. He believed that everything in our physical world was made up of earth, air, fire, and water.

Moving on, we have the Islamic Golden Age, where scientific enlightenment was at its peak. Smartypants like Jabir ibn Hayyan, or Geber to his friends in the West, went full-on alchemist mode, trying to turn base metals into gold and unlock the mysteries of everlasting life. Now, these guys may seem a little out there to us modern folk, but they were actually laying down the groundwork for the chemistry we know today.

As we leave the Middle Ages behind, we find ourselves in the Renaissance, where alchemists were breaking boundaries like nobody's business. Take Paracelsus, for instance - this dude was all about pushing the limits of his craft. With his mind-blowing experiments and out-of-the-box theories, he completely rocked both medicine and chemistry, changing the game forever.

But it wasn't until the Age of Enlightenment that things really took off. Heroes like Robert Boyle and Antoine Lavoisier were making major moves, conducting meticulous experiments and creating the laws that govern chemical reactions. Lavoisier, in particular, was all about combustion and oxygen, and his breakthroughs completely revolutionized the field, earning him the title of the father of modern chemistry.

The 19th century was a total explosion of scientific progress, my friend. Legends like John Dalton and Dmitri Mendeleev refined the atomic theory and put together the periodic table of elements, respectively. Countless other scientists, like Humphry Davy and Marie Curie, went all-in on studying matter, pushing our knowledge and smashing through the limits of what we thought was possible.

And here we are, on the edge of the 21st century, armed with a mind-boggling amount of knowledge and technology. From discovering new elements to creating life-saving drugs, chemistry has been shaping our world in ways that boggle the mind.

So, my fellow chemistry adventurers, let's embrace the legacy of the past and the endless possibilities of the future. In the pages ahead, we're gonna dive into the fundamental concepts, explore the wonders of the periodic table, and unlock the mysteries of chemical reactions. Together, we'll light the flame of curiosity, because the world of chemistry is waiting for us to uncover its secrets. Let's do this!

Physics

Alright, buckle up folks, because I'm about to take you on a wild, mind-bending adventure into the world of physics. Step 1 is all about laying that rock-solid foundation of knowledge. We're talking about really getting those fundamental concepts down pat because they're the building blocks for everything else. No shaky ground here, my friends. Our study guide gives you crystal-clear explanations and real-life examples that'll make those core principles stick in your noggin like glue.

Now, let's dive into step 2, where things start to get exciting. We're going to crack open Isaac Newton's laws of motion. This is the stuff that made him famous and forever changed the game of physics. But hey, we're not just going to give you some snooze-fest explanation. Oh no, we're going to show you just how elegant and beautiful these laws truly are. With jaw-dropping visuals, interactive exercises, and mind-blowing real-world examples, you'll start to see how objects move and dance with each other in ways you never thought possible.

Step 3? Buckle up, because we're talking about energy. Yeah, that thing that powers pretty much everything in the universe. We're going to guide you through the intricate world of energy and its crazy transformations. Like a tightrope walker, we'll delicately navigate the ins and outs of heat transfer and the mind-bending conversion of potential energy to kinetic energy. Trust me, when you're done with this step, you'll have a mind-blowing understanding of this abstract, invisible force that's everywhere around us.

Moving on to step 4, we're going to dive deep into the tantalizing world of electricity and magnetism. Prepare to be shocked and amazed by the invisible forces that make our world go round. We'll start by unraveling the secrets behind electric charges, and then we'll explore the incredible applications of electromagnetic waves. You'll be the one enlightening your friends at parties about all the super cool stuff you've learned in this step.

Hold on tight, because step 5 is like strapping yourself into a rocket and blasting off into the mind-bending realm of quantum mechanics. This is where reality gets thrown out the window and replaced by some seriously mind-boggling weirdness. It's like Alice falling down the rabbit hole, but instead of tea parties and mad hatters, you'll be diving into thought experiments and mind-bending questions. Trust me, you won't look at the world the same way after this step.

And finally, in step 6, we're bringing all this mind-bending stuff back down to Earth. Because hey, physics isn't just a lab experiment or something you read about in textbooks. No, this stuff is real and it affects every little bit of our everyday lives. From how your phone charges to how balls fly in sports, our study guide shows you how physics is literally everywhere. So you won't just be acing exams, you'll have a whole new appreciation for the subject and how it connects to the real world.

So, my fellow physics enthusiasts and curious minds, get ready for the ride of a lifetime. This step-by-step guide from Test Treasure Publication will transform how you see and understand the mind-blowing universe we live in. We're inviting all aspiring physicists, engineers, and anyone who's just plain curious to join us on this exhilarating journey. We'll unlock the secrets of the universe, one mind-expanding concept at a time. Are you in?

Geology

Are you ready to dive into the captivating world of geology? Trust me, it's a wild ride. We're about to unravel the mysteries of the Earth's structure, composition, and processes that have been puzzling scientists for ages. Get ready to embark on a journey that'll take you to the very depths of our planet. I'm talking about exploring its mind-blowing history and the crazy forces that have shaped it over countless years.

Alright, let's kick things off with Step 2: Earth's Formation and Evolution. It's like we're time travelers, going back to the birth of our planet and uncovering the incredible story of how it came to be. We'll witness the molten beginnings of the Earth and the development of its tectonic plates. Imagine each layer of this epic tale being unveiled right before your eyes. It's gonna be like a movie, but better, trust me.

Now, hold on tight for Step 3: Rocks and Minerals. We're about to decipher the secret language written in stone. It's like going on a virtual journey through the Earth's crust as we explore the crystal-like matrix of minerals and the insane variety of rocks that cover our planet. You won't believe the beauty of gemstones and the rugged toughness of igneous rocks until you see it for yourself. Seriously, every stone has a unique story to tell, and we're about to uncover it.

Step 4 is where it gets really exciting — Plate Tectonics. Get ready for a thrilling expedition through the Earth's ever-moving crust. We're diving headfirst into the mind-blowing concept of plate tectonics, where continents collide and rifts expand, forever changing our world. And guess what? We've got detailed explanations and stunning visuals to help you witness the raw power of earthquakes and volcanic eruptions. You'll walk away with a deep understanding of the forces that continue to shape our ever-changing planet.

But hold your breath, 'cause things get even more intense in Step 5: Earthquakes and Volcanoes. We're gonna explore the mind-blowing power of these natural disasters. It might be destructive, but man, it's mesmerizing. We're about to unravel the science behind these forces of nature that leave us in awe. From the unpredictable rumblings beneath the Earth's crust to the explosive eruptions that reshape entire landscapes, you won't help but appreciate the delicate balance between the Earth's fiery core and its fragile surface. Seriously, it's a wild dance that keeps us all on our toes.

In Step 6, buckle up for a face-to-face encounter with weathering, erosion, and deposition. Yeah, we're talking about the relentless forces that transform landscapes over time. Picture wind, water, ice, and gravity teaming up to sculpt and shape the Earth's surface. Glacier action, river valleys, it's all here. Nature's artistic hand is at work, and it's truly a sight to behold. Get ready to witness the intricate beauty of this constant dance between land and water.

And now it's time for Step 7: Geologic Time Scale. Brace yourselves. We're about to journey through the annals of time, exploring the mind-blowing world of geological history. Yeah, we're talking about the bigger picture here — from the origin of the Earth all the way to the present day. We're gonna dive into engaging narratives and visually stunning representations that'll make you appreciate the sheer magnitude of our planet's history. And hey, we'll even throw in some context to help you understand where humanity fits into all this geological time stuff. Pretty cool, huh?

Finally, in Step 8, we're gonna focus on the Earth's valuable resources. This is where things get real, my friend. We're gonna dive into everything from precious metals to fossil fuels and explore how they shape our modern lives. But wait, there's more! We'll also delve into the complexities of extracting and managing these resources sustainably. It's all about finding that delicate balance between our needs and the preservation of our planet's ecological integrity. We've got to be responsible.

So buckle up and get ready for the most epic journey through geology. Trust me, Test Treasure Publication is gonna take you beyond the surface of boring old rocks and immerse you in a world of wonder and discovery. Each step of this adventure is meticulously crafted to ignite your passion for the Earth sciences and give you the knowledge and understanding to excel in the FTCE Elementary Education K-6 exam. So come on, join us as we uncover the hidden treasures buried deep within the Earth. Get ready for an educational experience that'll blow your mind and transcend the ordinary.

Biology

Let me take you on a journey through time, to the ancient civilizations of Egypt and Mesopotamia. Picture it: the dust settling on the grand pyramids, the mighty rivers flowing, and the people, both physicians and philosophers, striving to unlock the enigmatic secrets of existence. Among them, a towering figure emerges – Imhotep, the legendary Egyptian physician. He's a trailblazer, you know, trailblazer in the field of medicine, and even biology. He was the fancy-pants who first started observing the human body and how it all works. That was like the foundation for all those fancy anatomical studies we have today. It's pretty impressive when you think about it, isn't it?

And then, we hop, skip, and jump ahead to Greece during its golden age, where it seemed like everyone and their grandmother was a thinker or scholar. It was a time when minds had no limits, and two big names come to mind – Hippocrates and Aristotle. Hippocrates, the father of medicine (what a title!), had this wild idea about how our health and disease were all related to the balance of bodily fluids. He nailed it, didn't he? And then there's Aristotle, diving into the natural world headfirst. He was like an ancient biologist, studying everything from structures to behaviors. He pretty much got the ball rolling for taxonomy, you know, the system we use to classify all living things today. It's like those two had a playdate with destiny and were all like, "Let's change biology forever!"

Now, brace yourself, my friend, for the Renaissance. It's an era of artistic and scientific enlightenment. Here comes Leonardo da Vinci, this genius artist who dives into dissections and meticulously sketches the human body. His drawings? They open our eyes to the intricacies of anatomy. It's like he's giving us a backstage pass to the human form, revealing all its secrets. I mean, who knew our insides could be so mesmerizing?

As we twirl through the 18th and 19th centuries, we witness a true awakening in biology. The rockstars of this era are Carl Linnaeus and Charles Darwin. Linnaeus, the king of classification – he was all about bringing order to the chaotic world of organisms. He gave them fancy names and put them in neat little boxes. It's like he created a universal language for biologists everywhere. And then, Darwin, oh boy, his theory of evolution shook things up. He challenged all those traditional beliefs about the origin of life and brought a whole new twist to the game. I mean, who knew we were all just products of this crazy thing called adaptation? It's really mind-blowing when you think about it.

Fast forward to the 20th and 21st centuries, oh man, biology is on turbo speed now. We got the discovery of this thing called DNA, thanks to James Watson, Francis Crick, and Rosalind Franklin. It's like they unlocked the blueprint of life, revealing those hidden secrets of genetics and molecular biology. Suddenly, it's a game-changer. We're talking genetic engineering and personalized medicine, my friend. It's like we're living in a sci-fi movie!

But wait, let's not forget about the unsung heroes of biology. These are the men and women who dedicated their lives to uncovering the mysteries of life. From Gregor Mendel, who did all those entertaining experiments with pea plants, to Jane Goodall, who spent day in and day out observing those fascinating chimpanzees. They're true MVPs, expanding our understanding of life in ways we never thought possible.

So here we stand, at the edge of this vast and awe-inspiring world of biology. Let's not shy away, my friend, let's embrace it with open arms. It's a realm where we discover the mysteries of our own existence. It's through this lens that we begin to realize just how deeply interconnected all living beings truly are. It's profound, it's mind-boggling, and it's the essence of what makes us human.

4

MATHEMATICS

Rational Numbers

Come on, let's take a trip back in time and dig into the beginnings of rational numbers. Picture this: we land in ancient Greece, where all the big shots like Pythagoras, Euclid, and Plato used to hang out. These guys were like the OG philosophers, always deep in thought, trying to wrap their heads around the secrets of the universe. And it was right here in Greece that the groundwork for rational numbers was laid, as these smarty pants philosophers went in deep, trying to figure out how numbers were all connected.

So first up we've got Pythagoras, the man, the myth, the mathematician. He was one of the first to try and nail down what rational numbers were all about. Check it - in his famous Pythagorean theorem, he was dealing with whole numbers. But this dude couldn't help but notice that square roots were a real mysterious thing. And guess what? That led him to discover these irrational numbers that couldn't be written as fractions. Mind-blowing, right?

Then along came Euclid, who dropped the ultimate knowledge bomb with his book "Elements." That bad boy became a math bible for ages. In there, Euclid brought ratios into the mix, basically laying down the foundation for us to understand rational numbers as fractions. It was like he had everything figured out, with his logical reasoning and precise proofs. He set the bar high for mathematicians to come.

Okay, fast forward to the Islamic Golden Age. This was when all the cool kids in the world of mathematics were hanging out. We're talking Al-Khwarizmi, Al-Jabr (who, by the way, is where the word "algebra" comes from), and a whole gang of other brilliant minds. These guys took Euclid's ideas and ran wild, introducing the world to decimal fractions and even infinite series. Mind-boggling stuff, my friend.

And who could forget the Renaissance? Talk about a game-changer. It was during this time that Fibonacci rolled in, bringing those Hindu-Arabic numerals to the Western world. It was like he was saying, "Hey guys, forget all those messy Roman numerals, these beauties are here to stay." And guess what? It made working with rational numbers way easier. A true hero, that Fibonacci.

Fast-forward a bit more, and we've got the 19th and 20th century math geniuses like Dedekind, Cantor, and Russell stealing the show. These guys took irrational numbers to a whole new level, pushing the boundaries of mathematical discourse. They basically uncovered the secrets of number theory and showed us just how complex and infinite the number world is.

Now, here we are in the present day. Rational numbers are still rockin' the math world, playing a big role in just about every aspect of our lives. We may not realize it, but they're all up in our everyday activities. Like when we're figuring out proportions, calculating probabilities, or trying to make sense of our finances. Rational numbers are like silent partners in our existence.

So, as you enter into the world of elementary education, it's important to really get the significance and depth of rational numbers. They hold the key to unlocking a whole new level of math understanding. But hey, don't sweat it. Test Treasure Publication is here to be your guide on this wild journey. We've got the knowledge and resources to help you navigate the rational number maze and hopefully ignite a lifelong love affair with math. Let's get this adventure started!

Equations

Welcome to the amazing world of equations, my friend. It's like stepping into a whole new universe, where numbers come alive and dance together in a symphony of symbols and signs. But don't worry, I've got your back. I'm here to guide you through this magical journey and give you the tools you need to unravel the mysteries of equations, one step at a time.

First things first, we need to understand the language these equations are speaking. It's like a secret code that we have to crack. From the humble equals sign to those mysterious exponents, every symbol has a role to play in this grand equation symphony. We'll break it down, dissect it, and reveal the hidden meanings behind each symbol.

Once we've got a handle on the language, it's time to find balance. Just like a tightrope walker on a slender rope, we need to make sure both sides of the equation are equal. It's all about finding that perfect harmony, where two scales are perfectly aligned. And we'll explore all the tricks and techniques to manipulate equations, from adding and subtracting to multiplying and dividing. With each move, we'll get closer to unveiling the answers hidden within the dance of the equation.

But that's not all, my friend. We're not just here to solve equations, we're here to unlock hidden treasures. Imagine yourself as a treasure hunter, on a thrilling quest to find that chest full of unknowns. Armed with our newfound equation knowledge, we'll venture into the realm of solving for variables. We'll substitute, simplify, and rearrange, until we uncover the solutions that were once shrouded in mystery. It'll take perseverance and strategic thinking, but we'll emerge victorious, with the treasures of the mathematical labyrinth in our hands.

Equations may have been born in the abstract world of numbers, but they have real-world implications too. That's why we'll take a detour and explore the practical side of equations. We'll calculate distances, determine finances, and dive into the diverse landscapes where equations play a vital role. It's all about bridging the gap between theory and reality, and empowering ourselves to see the world through the lens of mathematics.

Now, my friend, brace yourself for the final frontier. We're not satisfied with just basic equations. Oh no, we're going deep into the advanced territory. Quadratic equations, polynomials, exponential and logarithmic equations – nothing will stop us. We'll unravel their intricacies, conquer their challenges, and expand our mathematical prowess. We'll become masters of equations, reserved only for the brave souls who dare to venture into this realm.

Equations, my friend, are captivating and elusive. They whisper their secrets only to those who are courageous enough to untangle their enigmatic dance. But fear not, because with me as your trusted companion, you'll dive headfirst into this realm of mathematical wonder. You'll embrace the elegance of equations and unlock the boundless possibilities of the numerical world. Get ready, my friend, because this journey is about to begin, and it's going to be one for the books.

Inequalities

Welcome, my fellow adventurers, to the wonderful world of inequalities. Just like a skilled mountaineer studying the terrain before the climb, we're going to dive deep into the heart of inequalities. We'll uncover their purpose and explore why they're such a significant part of mathematical reasoning. It's all about equipping ourselves with a solid foundation, so we truly understand the principles that govern these inequalities.

Now, inequalities are like the diverse ecosystems we find on mountains. They come in all sorts of forms and structures, just like the various types of inequalities we'll be exploring in our second step. From the simple greater-than and less-than symbols to the more complex compound and absolute value inequalities, we'll dissect each one and guide you through the intricacies of solving them with precision and accuracy. Think of it as becoming an expert in navigating the different landscapes of inequalities.

Let's take a moment to imagine standing on a mountaintop, taking in the breathtaking vista below. That's the kind of beauty and vibrancy we want to bring to inequalities. In our third step, we're going to teach you how to see them as vibrant landscapes that can be graphically represented. We'll unravel the art of graphing inequalities, showing you techniques and strategies that'll allow you to visually interpret the solutions. Through vivid illustrations and step-by-step examples, we'll empower you to breathe life into these mathematical inequalities.

Now, solving inequalities is no easy feat. It's like navigating treacherous paths, just like a mountaineer would do to reach the summit. That's why, in our fourth step, we're going to equip you with a whole repertoire of problem-solving techniques. Whether it's using properties of inequality or applying algebraic reasoning, we'll explore each method meticulously and explain them in a way that's easy to grasp. With our guidance, you'll become a master at unraveling the complexity of inequalities with clarity and precision.

And as we conquer the mathematical heights together, we'll discover that inequalities extend far beyond just math. In our final step, we'll shed light on their practical applications in everyday life. We'll show you how inequalities can help you interpret data and make informed decisions. We'll guide you through exercises that bridge the gap between theoretical knowledge and real-world situations. It's about embracing the relevance and power of inequalities in our daily lives.

So, my friends, by the time we reach the end of our journey, you'll emerge as confident and skilled explorers of inequalities. Our adventure together will give you the necessary tools to navigate this intricate mathematical landscape. It'll ignite your curiosity and foster a deep understanding of this fundamental concept. And remember, at Test Treasure Publication, we go beyond the ordinary. We're your guides as we dive into the depths of mathematical reasoning and unlock your potential for extraordinary success. Together, we'll embark on a journey that not only prepares you for the FTCE Elementary Education K-6 exam but also instills a passion for lifelong learning. Join us, and let's embrace the wonders of inequalities!

Basic Functions

Come on in and let's fuel that fire of yours for the subject. We're gonna break down the whole shebang on understanding and using those basic functions. Our study materials are like having a personal mentor by your side, helping you wrap your head around these crucial mathematical operations.

First things first, we're gonna demystify addition. We'll show you how combining multiple quantities adds up to a sum. And trust me, we're not just gonna hit you with abstract concepts. We'll bring it down to earth with real-life examples and fun exercises that'll make you see the power of addition in everyday situations.

Now, let's venture into the exciting world of subtraction. This is where we reveal the ins and outs of taking something away to find the difference. We'll bring subtraction to life with relatable scenarios and hands-on activities that'll have you hooked and curious to know more.

Get ready for multiplication, a fancy way of saying repeated addition. We'll hold your hand and explore all the properties and principles behind this operation. Our goal is to go beyond just memorizing and help you truly understand how multiplication expands your math skills.

And last but not least, division. This is all about sharing or dividing a quantity equally. We're gonna unravel the secrets of dividing one number into smaller parts, so you'll have the tools to tackle even the trickiest numerical challenges. Get ready for thought-provoking examples and engaging activities that'll turn you into a division master.

At Test Treasure Publication, we know that true mastery of these basic functions goes way beyond memorization. Our study guide digs deep, igniting a love for math that'll carry you through life. We've crafted every page, exercise, and example to encourage critical thinking, problem-solving, and a thirst for learning that'll stick with you.

Remember, this is more than just prepping for a test. You're investing in your future. By mastering these essential operations, you're building a foundation for success in all the advanced math stuff and beyond.

So join us on this journey to extraordinary success in basic functions. Let's embark on a discovery that's gonna take your learning to a whole new level. At Test Treasure Publication, we'll be right there by your side, guiding you every step of the way.

Advanced Functions

Welcome aboard this thrilling adventure into the intricate world of advanced functions. Get ready to embark on a journey of self-discovery as we dive deep into the core challenges that students face when tackling these mind-boggling equations. We understand the frustration that bubbles up when faced with abstract concepts and complex equations, but fear not! We're here to be your trusty guides, equipping you with the necessary tools to conquer even the most daunting of equations.

Through clear explanations and real-life examples, we'll take the mystery out of functions, revealing their hidden patterns and principles. Brace yourself as we unveil the power of function notation, enabling you to express mathematical relationships with crystal-clear precision. And that's not all! We'll delve into the mesmerizing world of inverses and compositions, uncovering how these mathematical entities dance together and empowering you to confidently navigate through the intricate maze of function transformations.

But don't be fooled, our exploration doesn't stop at understanding functions. In this chapter, we unleash the true potential of advanced functions, bringing them to life in a myriad of real-world scenarios. From modeling financial investments to decoding biological phenomena, you'll witness firsthand how the concepts of functions weave their magic into every aspect of our lives. Our mission is to equip you not just with the skills to solve mathematical problems, but also with the ability to appreciate the profound impact that functions have on shaping the world around us.

Beyond the theoretical foundations, we're all about critical thinking and problem-solving. As you immerse yourself in the enchanting world of advanced functions, we're going to challenge you to think outside the box, encouraging you to unleash your creative problem-solving skills. Brace yourself for thought-provoking exercises and real-life scenarios that will inspire you to apply your newfound knowledge in innovative ways. Get ready to ignite your intellectual curiosity and nurture your independent thinking skills.

But hey, we know that everyone learns differently, which is why our study materials are designed to cater to all types of learners. We've got interactive online modules and visual representations galore, ensuring that your learning experience is personalized, engaging, and oh so fun. Because let's face it, we're all about igniting a passion for advanced functions that breaks all the traditional barriers of education.

As you embark on this thrilling expedition through advanced functions, be prepared to flex your analytical thinking, tune your mathematical intuition, and unlock the gateway to a realm of infinite possibilities. Armed with the knowledge and insight gained from this chapter, you'll not only conquer the challenges of advanced functions but also emerge as a confident and savvy problem solver.

So, join us, my friend, as we step into the boundless depths of advanced functions, illuminating a path of intellectual growth and unlocking your full mathematical potential. Together, let's embark on this transformative journey where the ordinary falls away, and extraordinary achievements await. Get ready for a ride unlike any other!

Probability

Step 1: Building a Solid Foundation

Alright, folks, let's start by laying down a solid foundation. Probability, my friends, is all about dealing with uncertainty using math. It's like a framework that helps us analyze and quantify the likelihood of things happening. And let me tell you, it's way more interesting and useful than you might think. We're talking about predicting weather, understanding stock market trends, and so much more. Once we truly get a grip on the fundamentals, we'll be able to navigate through the crazy world of probability with total confidence and precision.

Step 2: Getting to Know the Basics

Now that we're embarking on this wild journey, it's crucial for us to get familiar with some basic terms in the world of probability. You'll hear words like events, outcomes, sample spaces, and favorable outcomes thrown around a lot. Trust me, understanding these terms is gonna make communication a whole lot easier and help us navigate through the maze of probability with ease. Each one of these terms is like a treasure that's gonna light up our path and take us deeper into this amazing subject.

Step 3: Unleashing the Power of Probability Laws

Hold on tight, folks, 'cause we're about to dive into the captivating world of probability laws. These laws, like the Addition Rule and the Multiplication Rule, are like superpowers that give us the ability to calculate and analyze the chances of events happening, all in a super organized way. They're like keys that unlock the secrets hidden in probability and help us make sense even in the craziest of situations.

Step 4: Exploring Probability Distributions

Get ready for an adventure, my friends, as we journey into the fascinating realm of probability distributions. These distributions, like the famous Binomial Distribution or the fancy Normal Distribution, are gonna show us the patterns and characteristics of random variables. And why is that important, you ask? Well, understanding these distributions is gonna give us the power to interpret data and make smart decisions based on it. We're about to unleash the full potential of probability here, people!

Step 5: Becoming a Probability Master

Alright, folks, this is the final step in our epic quest. Buckle up as we dive straight into the art of probability modeling. We're gonna explore techniques like using tree diagrams, Venn diagrams, and something called Bayesian inference to model and solve real-life problems. It's like putting on a detective hat and unraveling all the mysteries hidden in the world of uncertainty. Once we embrace these tools, we'll be able to analyze tough situations, make predictions with confidence, and open up a whole new realm of possibilities.

With each step we take, my friends, we're getting closer to unraveling the mind-bending intricacies of probability. We're peeling back the layers of uncertainty to reveal the hidden treasures that lie beneath. Together, we'll become masters of probability, paving the way not just for academic success, but for a future full of limitless opportunities.

So come on, join me on this electrifying adventure through the world of probability. Together, we'll light up the path to extraordinary success. We'll take the ordinary and turn it into something extraordinary. We'll transform the unknown into a world of boundless possibilities. Buckle up, my friends, 'cause this journey is gonna be one heck of a wild ride!

Two-Dimensional Shapes

Step 1: Getting the Basics

Alright, folks, here we go. First things first, we gotta wrap our heads around the basic concepts of two-dimensional shapes. Get ready to dive into the language of geometry, my friends. We'll be getting cozy with terms like vertices, angles, and sides. These little nuggets of knowledge are gonna be our guide as we navigate through the wild world of shapes. Trust me, once we've got these basics down pat, we'll be strutting through this geometric playground like pros.

Step 2: Figuring Out Shapes

Now that we've got the basics locked and loaded, it's time to unravel the secrets of different two-dimensional shapes. We're talking about the elegant simplicity of triangles and the mind-boggling symmetries of regular polygons. Each shape has its own special features, my friends, and we're gonna dive deep into 'em. We'll be checking out detailed illustrations and doing interactive exercises to really wrap our heads around these properties. Soon enough, we'll be spotting shapes left and right, and we'll be able to compare and classify 'em with ease.

Step 3: Letting Our Creativity Loose

Listen up, folks, shapes aren't just for textbooks and boring equations. They've got a fiery spirit that lives in the world of art and design. Now, in this step, we're gonna let our imaginations run wild as we explore how shapes can be combined, twisted, and transformed into mind-blowing visual masterpieces. We're diving into the magical realm of tessellations, where shapes weave together in a beautiful dance. We'll also be getting our groove on with congruence, creating some seriously satisfying symmetrical creations. Get ready to unleash your inner artist, my friends, it's gonna be a wild ride.

Step 4: Making Real Connections

Shapes aren't just pretty things on paper, my friends. They've got a serious impact on the world around us. In this step, we'll be uncovering the practical applications of two-dimensional shapes in our everyday lives. We're talking about architecture, fashion design, product packaging, and even computer graphics. We'll be digging into real-world examples and getting those brains of ours churning with thought experiments. By making connections between abstract math and our tangible world, we'll gain a deeper appreciation for the role shapes play in shaping our environment. It's gonna blow your mind, folks.

Step 5: Reflecting and Applying

Alright, we're almost at the finish line, my friends. It's time to take a moment and reflect on everything we've learned so far. We'll be doing comprehensive review exercises and tackling some practice questions to really solidify our knowledge. But that's not all, folks. We're gonna put all that sweet expertise of ours to the test by solving some real-world problems. This is where we get to flex our shape-solving muscles and see just how powerful two-dimensional shapes are in analyzing, predicting, and creating. Get ready to show off what you've got, my friends.

Step 6: Becoming Masters and Beyond

Give yourselves a pat on the back, folks, 'cause we did it. We've conquered the world of two-dimensional shapes and laid the groundwork for a lifetime of geometric mastery. But hold on tight, 'cause this is just the beginning. Test Treasure Publication has a whole treasure trove of goodies waiting for us. We've got three-dimensional shapes and fancy-pants mathematical concepts just waiting to blow our minds. So let's embrace the challenges ahead, armed with the knowledge and confidence we've gained from our study of two-dimensional shapes. Get ready for a journey of learning and growth, my friends. We're gonna unlock the door to a world of endless possibilities.

Join us at Test Treasure Publication, where the extraordinary awaits and the ordinary fades away. Together, let's dive into the secrets of two-dimensional shapes and unlock a world of infinite possibilities.

5.1 Full-Length Practice Test 1

The Language Arts and Reading Section:

1. ELA Pedagogy:

Which of the following teaching strategies best supports students' reading comprehension?

A) Memorizing Text

B) Ignoring Unfamiliar Words

C) Reading Silently

D) Asking Open-Ended Questions

2. Foundations of Grammar:

What part of speech is the word "quickly" in the sentence "She quickly ran to the store"?

A) Adjective

B) Adverb

C) Noun

D) Preposition

3. Literary Analysis:

In literary analysis, what term refers to the central message or insight revealed through a literary work?

A) Tone

B) Theme

C) Setting

D) Plot

The Social Science Section:

4. U.S. History:

Who was the first President of the United States?

A) Thomas Jefferson

B) Benjamin Franklin

C) John Adams

D) George Washington

5. World History:

The ancient city of Rome was built on how many hills?

A) Three

B) Five

C) Seven

D) Nine

The Science Section:

6. Scientific Inquiry and Lab Safety:

In a scientific lab, what should you do if a chemical spills on your skin?

A) Wipe it off with a cloth

B) Wash with soap and water

C) Notify the teacher and follow instructions

D) Apply a bandage

7. Chemistry:

What is the atomic number of carbon?

A) 6

B) 8

C) 12

D) 14

The Mathematics Section:

8. Rational Numbers:

Which of the following is NOT a rational number?

A) 2/3

B) 0.75

C) $\sqrt{2}$

D) 4

9. Probability:

What is the probability of rolling a 3 on a fair six-sided die?

A) 1/3

B) 1/6

C) 1/2

D) 2/3

The Language Arts and Reading Section:

10. Vocabulary and Word Relationships:

What is the synonym of the word "benevolent"?

A) Malevolent

B) Kind

C) Hostile

D) Angry

11. Punctuation:

Which sentence is punctuated correctly?

A) "She said, "Let's go to the park.""

B) "She said, "Let's go to the park."

C) "She said, 'Let's go to the park.'"

D) "She said, Let's go to the park."

12. Reading Comprehension:

If the main idea of a passage is supported by details, what are these details referred to as?

A) Examples

B) Supporting Details

C) Topics

D) Themes

The Social Science Section:

13. Geography:

What is the largest continent by land area?

A) Africa

B) Asia

C) Europe

D) Australia

14. Civics and Citizenship:

What is the supreme law of the United States?

A) The Declaration of Independence

B) The Magna Carta

C) The U.S. Constitution

D) The Emancipation Proclamation

15. Economics:

What term refers to the total value of all goods and services produced within a country in a given period?

A) Inflation

B) Gross Domestic Product

C) Interest Rate

D) Trade Deficit

The Science Section:

16. Physics:

What force opposes motion between two surfaces that are touching?

A) Gravity

B) Friction

C) Inertia

D) Momentum

17. Geology:

What type of rock is formed from cooled and solidified magma?

A) Sedimentary

B) Metamorphic

C) Igneous

D) Mineral

The Mathematics Section:

18. Equations:

What is the value of x in the equation 2x + 3 = 9?

A) 1

B) 2

C) 3

D) 4

19. Two-Dimensional Shapes:

What is the area of a rectangle with a length of 10 units and a width of 5 units?

A) 15

B) 25

C) 50

D) 100

20. Basic Functions:

If f(x) = 2x + 5, what is f(3)?

A) 11

B) 16

C) 8

D) 21

21. Inequalities:

Which of the following represents the solution to the inequality 2x - 5 > 3?

A) x > 4

B) x < 4

C) x > -4

D) x < -4

22. Advanced Functions:

What is the derivative of the function f(x) = 3x^2 - 4x + 7?

A) 3x - 4

B) 6x - 4

C) 6x + 4

D) 3x + 4

23. Biology:

What cellular organelle is responsible for producing ATP?

A) Nucleus

B) Ribosome

C) Mitochondrion

D) Endoplasmic Reticulum

24. Agreement and Sentence Structure:

Which of the following sentences is grammatically correct?

A) She neither likes coffee or tea.

B) She likes neither coffee or tea.

C) She neither likes coffee nor tea.

D) She likes neither coffee nor tea.

25. Probability:

A bag contains 3 red marbles, 4 blue marbles, and 5 green marbles. What is the probability of drawing a red marble?

A) 1/4

B) 3/12

C) 3/7

D) 3/5

The Language Arts and Reading Section:

26. Literary Analysis:

What literary device is used when words are repeated at the beginning of successive clauses?

A) Alliteration

B) Anaphora

C) Onomatopoeia

D) Simile

The Social Science Section:

27. U.S. History:

What amendment to the U.S. Constitution abolished slavery?

A) 10th Amendment

B) 13th Amendment

C) 15th Amendment

D) 18th Amendment

28. World History:

Which ancient civilization is known for building the Great Wall?

A) Greece

B) China

C) Egypt

D) Rome

The Science Section:

29. Chemistry:

What is the chemical symbol for gold?

A) Au

B) Ag

C) Go

D) Gd

30. Science, Technology, and Society:

Which type of renewable energy relies on flowing water?

A) Solar Power

B) Hydroelectric Power

C) Wind Power

D) Nuclear Power

The Mathematics Section:

31. Probability:

A die is rolled. What is the probability of rolling an even number?

A) 1/2

B) 1/3

C) 2/3

D) 1/4

32. Two-Dimensional Shapes:

What is the perimeter of a square with a side length of 6 units?

A) 12

B) 18

C) 24

D) 36

33. Equations:

If 3x + 2 = 11, what is the value of x?

A) 1

B) 2

C) 3

D) 4

34. Foundations of Grammar:

Which sentence is grammatically correct?

A) She's books are on the table.

B) Hers books are on the table.

C) Her books are on the table.

D) She book are on the table.

35. Punctuation:

Which of the following is punctuated correctly?

A) "Where are you going? she asked."

B) "Where are you going"? she asked.

C) "Where are you going?" She asked.

D) "Where are you going," she asked?

36. Social Studies Skills and Pedagogy:

In teaching social studies, what skill helps students understand relationships between locations?

A) Calculating

B) Map Reading

C) Memorizing Dates

D) Singing National Anthems

37. U.S. Government:

Who is the Commander-in-Chief of the U.S. military?

A) Secretary of Defense

B) The President

C) Chief Justice

D) Speaker of the House

38. Civics and Citizenship:

What is the minimum voting age in the United States?

A) 16

B) 17

C) 18

D) 21

39. Economics:

What is a market economy primarily driven by?

A) Government Regulations

B) Supply and Demand

C) Fixed Prices

D) Central Planning

40. Scientific Inquiry and Lab Safety:

What should you do if a chemical splashes in your eyes in a lab?

A) Wipe your eyes with a cloth

B) Rinse with water immediately

C) Continue the experiment

D) Wait for instructions

41. Geology:

What type of rock is formed by the cooling and solidification of magma or lava?

A) Sedimentary

B) Igneous

C) Metamorphic

D) Mineral

42. Biology:

What is the process by which plants make food using sunlight?

A) Digestion

B) Respiration

C) Photosynthesis

D) Fermentation

43. Advanced Functions:

If $f(x)=x^2+2$, what is $f(3)$?

A) 9

B) 11

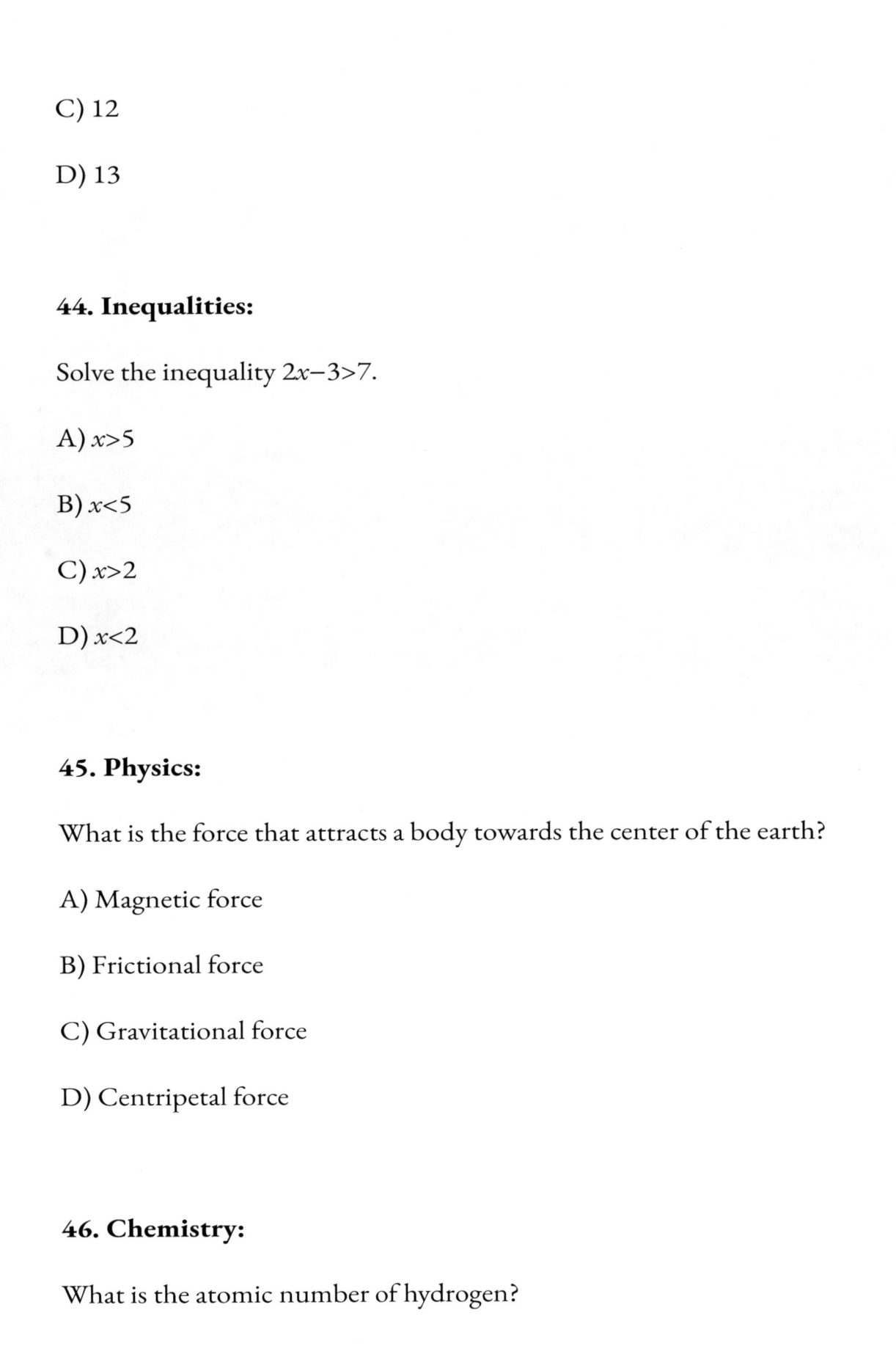

C) 12

D) 13

44. Inequalities:

Solve the inequality 2x−3>7.

A) x>5

B) x<5

C) x>2

D) x<2

45. Physics:

What is the force that attracts a body towards the center of the earth?

A) Magnetic force

B) Frictional force

C) Gravitational force

D) Centripetal force

46. Chemistry:

What is the atomic number of hydrogen?

A) 0

B) 1

C) 2

D) 3

47. Rational Numbers:

Which of the following is not a rational number?

A) 2/3

B) 5/4

C) $\sqrt{2}$

D) 8/2

48. Basic Functions:

If $g(x)=3x-4$, what is g(2)?

A) 1

B) 2

C) 4

D) 6

49. Vocabulary and Word Relationships:

Choose the word that is most opposite in meaning to "exuberant."

A) Reserved

B) Energetic

C) Joyful

D) Melancholic

50. Agreement and Sentence Structure:

Which sentence is grammatically correct?

A) He neither likes coffee or tea.

B) He neither likes coffee nor tea.

C) He neither likes coffee nor tea, either.

D) He likes neither coffee nor tea.

The Language Arts and Reading Section:

51. Reading Comprehension:

What is the main purpose of an introductory paragraph in an essay?

A) To provide supporting details

B) To present the thesis statement

C) To conclude the essay

D) To analyze the topic

52. Vocabulary and Word Relationships:

What is the antonym of "defeat"?

A) Success

B) Failure

C) Yield

D) Surrender

The Social Science Section:

53. Economics:

Which term refers to a general increase in prices and fall in the purchasing value of money?

A) Recession

B) Inflation

C) Deflation

D) Stagnation

54. Civics and Citizenship:

Which U.S. document contains the phrase "We the People"?

A) The Bill of Rights

B) The Articles of Confederation

C) The Preamble to the Constitution

D) The Emancipation Proclamation

The Science Section:

55. Physics:

What is the SI unit of force?

A) Joule

B) Newton

C) Watt

D) Volt

56. Biology:

What type of cells lack a nucleus?

A) Eukaryotic

B) Prokaryotic

C) Mitochondrial

D) Chloroplast

The Mathematics Section:

57. Basic Functions:

If $h(x)=2x-5$, what is $h(4)$?

A) 3

B) 4

C) 5

D) 6

58. Probability:

In a deck of 52 playing cards, what is the probability of drawing a red card?

A) 1/4

B) 1/2

C) 1/3

D) 2/3

59. Two-Dimensional Shapes:

What is the area of a circle with a radius of 3 units? (Use $\pi=3.14$)

A) 9.42

B) 18.84

C) 28.26

D) 37.68

60. Rational Numbers:

Which of the following numbers is an irrational number?

A) 5/8

B) $\sqrt{9}$

C) 2/3

D) π

61. Literary Analysis:

What is the perspective from which a story is told called?

A) Plot

B) Setting

C) Theme

D) Point of View

62. Punctuation:

Which of the following is punctuated correctly?

A) Its raining outside.

B) It's raining, outside.

C) It's raining outside.

D) Its' raining outside.

63. U.S. Government:

Who appoints federal judges in the United States?

A) Congress

B) The President

C) The Supreme Court

D) State Governors

64. U.S. History:

What was the main goal of the Civil Rights Movement in the United States?

A) Economic Prosperity

B) Equal Rights for All Citizens

C) Expansion of Territories

D) Establishment of a New Government

65. Social Studies Skills and Pedagogy:

What is the study of the Earth's physical features and how humans affect them called?

A) Biology

B) Geology

C) Geography

D) Anthropology

66. World History:

What was the main economic system in medieval Europe?

A) Capitalism

B) Socialism

C) Feudalism

D) Mercantilism

67. Geology:

What type of rock is formed from pre-existing rocks subjected to high heat and pressure?

A) Igneous

B) Sedimentary

C) Metamorphic

D) Limestone

68. Chemistry:

What is the chemical formula for water?

A) H_2O

B) O_2

C) $2CO_2$

D) N_2

69. Scientific Inquiry and Lab Safety:

What should you do if a chemical splashes in your eyes during a lab experiment?

A) Wipe with a cloth

B) Rinse with water

C) Use an eye dropper

D) Apply an ice pack

70. Equations:

What is the solution to the equation $2x-3=11$?

A) 4

B) 5

C) 6

D) 7

The Language Arts and Reading Section:

71. Literary Analysis:

What is the conflict in a story that takes place within a character's mind called?

A) External Conflict

B) Internal Conflict

C) Complex Conflict

D) Simple Conflict

72. Vocabulary and Word Relationships:

What type of words are used to show the relationship between the noun or pronoun and other words in a sentence?

A) Verbs

B) Prepositions

C) Adjectives

D) Adverbs

The Social Science Section:

73. Geography:

Which of the following oceans is the largest?

A) Atlantic Ocean

B) Indian Ocean

C) Southern Ocean

D) Pacific Ocean

74. U.S. Government:

What are the first ten amendments to the U.S. Constitution called?

A) The Bill of Rights

B) The Federalist Papers

C) The Articles of Confederation

D) The Preamble

The Science Section:

75. Biology:

In which cellular process does glucose react with oxygen to produce energy, carbon dioxide, and water?

A) Respiration

B) Digestion

C) Photosynthesis

D) Fermentation

76. Physics:

What is the term for the ability of an object to resist changes in its state of motion?

A) Momentum

B) Inertia

C) Velocity

D) Acceleration

The Mathematics Section:

77. Probability:

If you roll two six-sided dice, what is the probability of getting a sum of 7?

A) 1/6

B) 1/8

C) 1/12

D) 1/4

78. Equations:

What is the solution to the equation $x/3+2=5$?

A) 3

B) 6

C) 9

D) 12

79. Inequalities:

Which of the following is the solution set for the inequality $2x-3>1$?

A) $x>2$

B) $x<2$

C) $x>1$

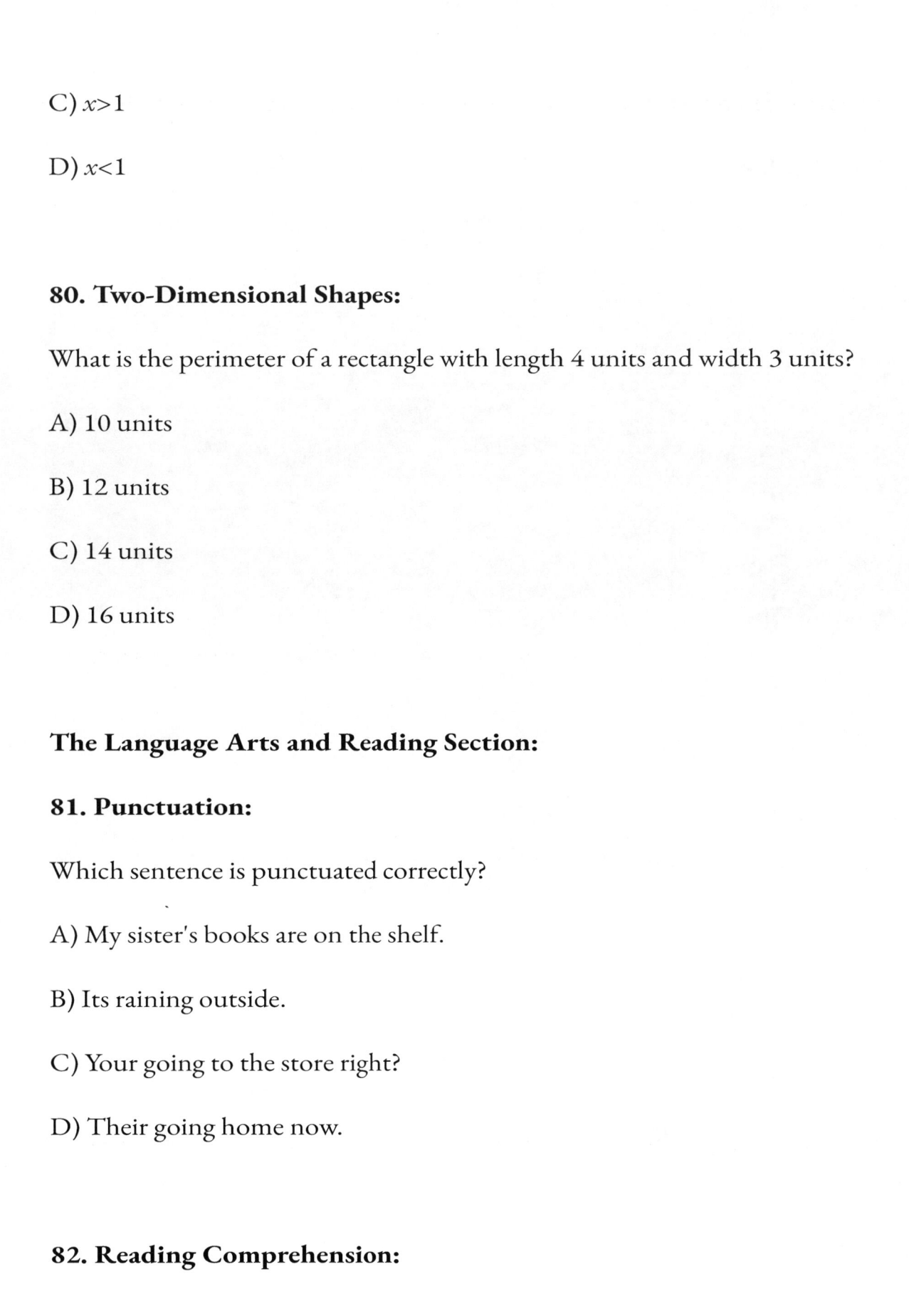

D) $x<1$

80. Two-Dimensional Shapes:

What is the perimeter of a rectangle with length 4 units and width 3 units?

A) 10 units

B) 12 units

C) 14 units

D) 16 units

The Language Arts and Reading Section:

81. Punctuation:

Which sentence is punctuated correctly?

A) My sister's books are on the shelf.

B) Its raining outside.

C) Your going to the store right?

D) Their going home now.

82. Reading Comprehension:

If a passage describes a character as "meticulous," what does this imply about the character?

A) Careless

B) Bold

C) Disorganized

D) Detail-oriented

The Social Science Section:

83. Economics:

What is the study of how people choose to use resources to satisfy their wants and needs called?

A) Sociology

B) Anthropology

C) Economics

D) Geography

84. Civics and Citizenship:

Which amendment to the U.S. Constitution grants the right to vote regardless of race?

A) 15th Amendment

B) 18th Amendment

C) 19th Amendment

D) 21st Amendment

The Science Section:

85. Geology:

What is the Earth's outermost layer called?

A) Core

B) Mantle

C) Crust

D) Lithosphere

86. Chemistry:

Which of the following is a noble gas?

A) Nitrogen (N)

B) Oxygen (O)

C) Helium (He)

D) Carbon (C)

The Mathematics Section:

87. Basic Functions:

What is the slope of the line given by the equation $y=2x+3$?

A) 0

B) 2

C) 3

D) -2

88. Advanced Functions:

What are the solutions to the quadratic equation $x^2-5x+6=0$?

A) $x=1,6$

B) $x=2,3$

C) $x=3,2$

D) $x=4,1$

89. Probability:

A bag contains 3 red, 2 blue, and 1 green ball. What is the probability of drawing a red ball?

A) 1/2

B) 1/3

C) 1/6

D) 2/3

90. Equations:

If $3x-4=8$, what is the value of x?

A) 2

B) 3

C) 4

D) 5

More Questions:

91. U.S. History:

Which U.S. President signed the Emancipation Proclamation?

A) George Washington

B) Thomas Jefferson

C) Abraham Lincoln

D) Theodore Roosevelt

92. Literary Analysis:

What literary device uses exaggeration for emphasis or effect?

A) Metaphor

B) Irony

C) Hyperbole

D) Alliteration

93. Physics:

What is the measure of the gravitational force between two objects called?

A) Tension

B) Weight

C) Mass

D) Friction

94. Social Studies Skills and Pedagogy:

What is a primary source in historical research?

A) A biography

B) A newspaper article

C) An encyclopedia entry

D) A letter from the time period

95. Two-Dimensional Shapes:

What is the area of a triangle with a base of 10 units and a height of 5 units?

A) 15 units^2

B) 25 units^2

C) 50 units^2

D) 75 units^2

The Language Arts and Reading Section:

96. Vocabulary and Word Relationships:

What is a synonym for "abundant"?

A) Scarce

B) Plentiful

C) Sparse

D) Meager

97. Agreement and Sentence Structure:

Which sentence correctly uses subject-verb agreement?

A) The dogs runs fast.

B) She enjoy reading.

C) They sings well.

D) The boy plays outside

The Social Science Section:

98. Geography:

What imaginary line divides the Earth into Northern and Southern Hemispheres?

A) Equator

B) Prime Meridian

C) Tropic of Cancer

D) Tropic of Capricorn

99. U.S. Government:

The U.S. Senate has how many members?

A) 100

B) 435

C) 50

D) 200

The Science Section:

100. Biology: What organelle is responsible for energy production in a cell?

A) Nucleus

B) Mitochondrion

C) Golgi Apparatus

D) Endoplasmic Reticulum

5.2 Answer Sheet - Practice Test 1

1. Answer: D

Explanation: Asking open-ended questions encourages students to think critically and engage with the text, enhancing comprehension.

2. Answer: B

Explanation: The word "quickly" describes how she ran, so it's an adverb.

3. Answer: B

Explanation: Theme refers to the central idea or message of a literary work.

4. Answer: D

Explanation: George Washington was the first President of the United States.

5. Answer: C

Explanation: Rome was famously built on seven hills.

6. Answer: C

Explanation: In the event of a chemical spill, it is essential to notify the teacher and follow their instructions, as they will know the correct procedure for that specific chemical.

7. Answer: A

Explanation: The atomic number of carbon, representing the number of protons in the nucleus, is 6.

8. Answer: C

Explanation: √2 is an irrational number because it cannot be expressed as a simple fraction.

9. Answer: B

Explanation: There is only one way to roll a 3 on a six-sided die, so the probability is 1 out of 6.

10. Answer: B

Explanation: "Benevolent" means well-meaning and kind, so the synonym is "kind."

11. Answer: C

Explanation: Option C correctly uses single quotation marks inside the double quotation marks.

12. Answer: B

Explanation: These details are known as supporting details.

13. Answer: B

Explanation: Asia is the largest continent by land area.

14. Answer: C

Explanation: The U.S. Constitution is considered the supreme law of the United States.

15. Answer: B

Explanation: Gross Domestic Product (GDP) measures the total value of all goods and services produced within a country.

16. Answer: B

Explanation: Friction is the force that opposes the motion between two surfaces in contact.

17. Answer: C

Explanation: Igneous rocks are formed from cooled and solidified magma.

18. Answer: C

Explanation: Subtract 3 from both sides to get 2x = 6, and then divide by 2 to find x = 3.

19. Answer: C

Explanation: The area of a rectangle is given by length × width, so the area is 10 × 5 = 50.

20. Answer: A

Explanation: Substitute x = 3 into the equation to find f(3) = 2(3) + 5 = 6 + 5 = 11.

21. Answer: A

Explanation: Add 5 to both sides, then divide by 2 to find x > 4.

22. Answer: B

Explanation: The derivative of 3x^2 is 6x, and the derivative of -4x is -4, so the answer is 6x - 4.

23. Answer: C

Explanation: The mitochondrion is known as the "powerhouse of the cell" and is responsible for producing ATP.

24. Answer: D

Explanation: The correct usage of "neither" is with "nor," as in "She likes neither coffee nor tea."

25. Answer: A

Explanation: There are 3 red marbles and 12 marbles in total, so the probability is 3/12, which simplifies to 1/4.

26. Answer: B

Explanation: Anaphora is the repetition of a word or phrase at the beginning of successive clauses.

27. Answer: B

Explanation: The 13th Amendment abolished slavery in the United States.

28. Answer: B

Explanation: The Great Wall was built by China.

29. Answer: A

Explanation: Au is the chemical symbol for gold.

30. Answer: B

Explanation: Hydroelectric power relies on flowing water.

31. Answer: A

Explanation: There are 3 even numbers on a standard die, so the probability is 3/6 = 1/2.

32. Answer: C

Explanation: The perimeter of a square is 4 times the length of one side, so the perimeter is 6 × 4 = 24.

33. Answer: C

Explanation: Subtract 2 from both sides and then divide by 3 to find x = 3.

34. Answer: C

Explanation: "Her books are on the table" is the correct sentence.

35. Answer: C

Explanation: Option C uses correct punctuation for a quoted question.

36. Answer: B

Explanation: Map reading helps students understand the relationships between locations.

37. Answer: B

Explanation: The President is the Commander-in-Chief of the U.S. military.

38. Answer: C

Explanation: The minimum voting age in the United States is 18.

39. Answer: B

Explanation: A market economy is primarily driven by supply and demand.

40. Answer: B

Explanation: If a chemical splashes in your eyes in a lab, you should rinse with water immediately.

41. Answer: B

Explanation: Igneous rock is formed by the cooling and solidification of magma or lava.

42. Answer: C

Explanation: Photosynthesis is the process by which plants make food using sunlight.

43. Answer: B

Explanation: $f(3)=3^2+2=9+2=11$.

44. Answer: A

Explanation: $2x-3>7$ implies $2x>10$ and $x>5$.

45. Answer: C

Explanation: The gravitational force attracts a body towards the center of the earth.

46. Answer: B

Explanation: The atomic number of hydrogen is 1.

47. Answer: C

Explanation: √2 is not a rational number, as it cannot be expressed as a simple fraction.

48. Answer: B

Explanation: $g(2)=3(2)-4=6-4=2$.

49. Answer: D

Explanation: "Exuberant" means extremely joyful or enthusiastic, while "melancholic" means sad or gloomy, making it the opposite.

50. Answer: D

Explanation: The correct usage of "neither" is with "nor," as in "He likes neither coffee nor tea."

51. Answer: B

Explanation: The introductory paragraph typically introduces the main idea or thesis statement of the essay.

52. Answer: A

Explanation: The antonym of "defeat" is "success."

53. Answer: B

Explanation: Inflation refers to a general increase in prices and a fall in the purchasing value of money.

54. Answer: C

Explanation: The phrase "We the People" is found in the Preamble to the Constitution.

55. Answer: B

Explanation: The SI unit of force is the Newton.

56. Answer: B

Explanation: Prokaryotic cells lack a nucleus.

57. Answer: A

Explanation: $h(4) = 2 \cdot 4 - 5 = 8 - 5 = 3$.

58. Answer: B

Explanation: There are 26 red cards in a standard deck, so the probability is $26/52 = 1/2$.

59. Answer: C

Explanation: The area of a circle is given by $\pi r^2 = 3.14 \times 3^2 = 3.14 \times 9 = 28.26$.

60. Answer: D

Explanation: π is an irrational number, as it cannot be expressed as a simple fraction.

61. Answer: D

Explanation: The perspective from which a story is told is called the Point of View.

62. Answer: C

Explanation: "It's raining outside." is punctuated correctly.

63. Answer: B

Explanation: The President appoints federal judges in the United States.

64. Answer: B

Explanation: The main goal of the Civil Rights Movement was to achieve equal rights for all citizens.

65. Answer: C

Explanation: Geography is the study of the Earth's physical features and how humans affect them.

66. Answer: C

Explanation: Feudalism was the main economic system in medieval Europe.

67. Answer: C

Explanation: Metamorphic rocks are formed from pre-existing rocks subjected to high heat and pressure.

68. Answer: A

Explanation: The chemical formula for water is $H2O$.

69. Answer: B

Explanation: If a chemical splashes in your eyes, you should rinse with water.

70. Answer: D

Explanation: $2x-3=11 \Longrightarrow 2x=14 \Longrightarrow x=7$.

71. Answer: B

Explanation: Internal Conflict is a psychological struggle within the character's mind.

72. Answer: B

Explanation: Prepositions are used to show the relationship between the noun or pronoun and other words in a sentence.

73. Answer: D

Explanation: The Pacific Ocean is the largest ocean on Earth.

74. Answer: A

Explanation: The first ten amendments to the U.S. Constitution are called the Bill of Rights.

75. Answer: A

Explanation: Cellular respiration involves the breakdown of glucose with the consumption of oxygen to produce energy, carbon dioxide, and water.

76. Answer: B

Explanation: Inertia is the ability of an object to resist changes in its state of motion.

77. Answer: A

Explanation: There are six possible outcomes that result in a sum of 7: (1, 6), (2, 5), (3, 4), (4, 3), (5, 2), (6, 1). Out of a total of 36 possible outcomes (6 faces on the first die multiplied by 6 faces on the second die), the probability is 6/36, which simplifies to 1/6.

78. Answer: C

Explanation: Solve for x: $x/3=3 \Longrightarrow x=9$.

79. Answer: A

Explanation: Solve for x: $2x>4 \Longrightarrow x>2$.

80. Answer: C

Explanation: The perimeter of a rectangle is given by $2 \times \text{length} + 2 \times \text{width} = 2 \times 4 + 2 \times 3 = 14$ units.

81. Answer: A

Explanation: Option A correctly uses the possessive apostrophe in "sister's."

82. Answer: D

Explanation: "Meticulous" describes someone who pays careful attention to detail.

83. Answer: C

Explanation: Economics studies how people choose to use resources to satisfy their wants and needs.

84. Answer: A

Explanation: The 15th Amendment grants the right to vote regardless of race.

85. Answer: C

Explanation: The Earth's outermost layer is called the crust.

86. Answer: C

Explanation: Helium is a noble gas and is chemically inert under normal conditions.

87. Answer: B

Explanation: The slope of the line is the coefficient of *x*, which is 2 in this case.

88. Answer: B

Explanation: The solutions to the quadratic equation can be found by factoring or using the quadratic formula, yielding $x=2,3$.

89. Answer: A

Explanation: There are 3 red balls out of a total of 6, so the probability is 3/6, or 1/2.

90. Answer: C

Explanation: Solving the equation: $3x-4=8 \Longrightarrow 3x=12 \Longrightarrow x=4$.

91. Answer: C

Explanation: Abraham Lincoln signed the Emancipation Proclamation.

92. Answer: C

Explanation: Hyperbole uses exaggeration for emphasis or effect.

93. Answer: B

Explanation: Weight is the measure of the gravitational force between two objects.

94. Answer: D

Explanation: A letter from the time period would be considered a primary source.

95. Answer: B

Explanation: The area of a triangle is given by 1/2×base×height=1/2×10×5=25.

96. Answer: B

Explanation: "Abundant" and "plentiful" both convey the idea of being present in large quantities.

97. Answer: D

Explanation: In option D, the subject and verb agree in number, making it grammatically correct.

98. Answer: A

Explanation: The Equator divides the Earth into Northern and Southern Hemispheres.

99. Answer: A

Explanation: The U.S. Senate is composed of 100 members, two from each state.

100. Answer: B

Explanation: The mitochondrion is responsible for energy production in a cell.

6.1 FULL-LENGTH PRACTICE TEST 2

The Science Section:

101. Scientific Inquiry and Lab Safety:

Which of the following should always be worn during a lab experiment to protect the eyes?

A) Gloves

B) Lab coat

C) Safety goggles

D) Earplugs

The Mathematics Section:

102. Probability:

If you flip a fair coin twice, what is the probability of getting two heads in a row?

A) 1/2

B) 1/3

C) 1/4

D) 1/8

103. Two-Dimensional Shapes:

What is the perimeter of a rectangle with a length of 8 units and a width of 4 units?

A) 24 units

B) 32 units

C) 12 units

D) 48 units

104. Equations:

Solve the equation $4x-5=11$ for x.

A) 1

B) 2

C) 3

D) 4

105. World History:

Who was the first Emperor of the Roman Empire?

A) Julius Caesar

B) Augustus Caesar

C) Nero

D) Marcus Aurelius

106. Civics and Citizenship:

What is the main duty of the judicial branch of the U.S. government?

A) Enforce laws

B) Make laws

C) Interpret laws

D) Collect taxes

107. Physics:

Which SI unit is used to measure luminous intensity?

A) Candela (cd)

B) Lux (lx)

C) Watt (W)

D) Joule (J)

108. Chemistry:

Which element is represented by the chemical symbol Na?

A) Nickel

B) Sodium

C) Nitrogen

D) Neptunium

109. Inequalities:

If 5x<15, what are the possible values for x?

A) x<3

B) x≤3

C) x>3

D) x≥3

110. Advanced Functions:

What is the derivative of the function f(x)=3x^2−2x+5?

A) 6x−2

B) 6x+2

C) 3x^2+5

D) 3x−5

The Language Arts and Reading Section:

111. Literary Analysis:

Which literary device is used in the phrase "Time flies when you're having fun"?

A) Metaphor

B) Alliteration

C) Onomatopoeia

D) Hyperbole

The Social Science Section:

112. Economics:

The law of supply states that, all else being equal, an increase in price results in what?

A) Decrease in quantity supplied

B) Increase in quantity supplied

C) Decrease in demand

D) Increase in demand

The Science Section:

113. Geology:

Which layer of the Earth is primarily composed of solid iron and nickel?

A) Crust

B) Mantle

C) Outer core

D) Inner core

114. Science, Technology, and Society:

Which renewable energy source derives power from the heat stored in Earth's interior?

A) Solar

B) Wind

C) Geothermal

D) Hydroelectric

The Mathematics Section:

115. Basic Functions:

The slope of a horizontal line is:

A) 0

B) Undefined

C) 1

D) -1

116. Rational Numbers:

If 5/2 is added to 1/3, what is the result?

A) 11/6

B) 7/6

C) 8/5

D) 3/2

117. Civics and Citizenship:

Which amendment to the U.S. Constitution guarantees freedom of speech?

A) First Amendment

B) Second Amendment

C) Third Amendment

D) Fourth Amendment

118. Physics:

What is the acceleration due to gravity on the surface of the Earth?

A) 9.8 m/s^2

B) 9.8 m/s

C) 10 m/s^2

D) 10 m/s

119. U.S. History:

What was the main cause of the American Revolutionary War?

A) Slavery

B) Territorial disputes

C) Taxation without representation

D) Religious conflicts

120. Chemistry:

What does the atomic number of an element represent?

A) Total number of protons and neutrons

B) Total number of protons

C) Total number of electrons

D) Total mass of the atom

121. Punctuation:

Which of the following sentences uses a semicolon correctly?

A) The cake is ready; to eat.

B) The cake is ready; let's eat it.

C) The cake is ready, let's eat; it.

D) The cake; is ready to eat.

122. Geography:

What is the capital city of France?

A) London

B) Madrid

C) Rome

D) Paris

123. Biology:

Which organ in the human body is responsible for detoxification?

A) Heart

B) Liver

C) Kidneys

D) Lungs

124. Equations:

Solve the equation $5x+2=17$ for x.

A) 1

B) 2

C) 3

D) 4

125. Literary Analysis:

In literature, what does the term "theme" refer to?

A) The main character

B) The setting of the story

C) The central idea or message

D) The plot

126. World History:

Who was the first female Prime Minister of the United Kingdom?

A) Margaret Thatcher

B) Theresa May

C) Queen Elizabeth II

D) Angela Merkel

127. Inequalities:

Which inequality represents "five times a number is at least 15"?

A) $5x \leq 15$

B) $5x \geq 15$

C) $x \leq 15$

D) $5x \geq 15$

128. U.S. Government:

What is the minimum age requirement to become President of the United States?

A) 25

B) 30

C) 35

D) 40

129. Two-Dimensional Shapes:

What is the area of a triangle with a base of 10 units and a height of 5 units?

A) 25 square units

B) 50 square units

C) 15 square units

D) 30 square units

130. Vocabulary and Word Relationships:

What is the synonym for "Ubiquitous"?

A) Rare

B) Common

C) Limited

D) Scarce

131. Economics:

What is a market economy primarily guided by?

A) Government regulations

B) Supply and demand

C) Religious principles

D) Tradition

132. Advanced Functions:

If $f(x)=x^2+2x-3$, what is $f(-1)$?

A) 0

B) −4

C) 4

D) -6

133. Probability:

If you roll a fair six-sided die, what is the probability of rolling a number greater than 4?

A) 1/3

B) 1/2

C) 1/6

D) 1/4

134. Scientific Inquiry and Lab Safety:

Why is it important to wear safety goggles in a laboratory setting?

A) To look professional

B) To protect the eyes from harmful chemicals or objects

C) To improve vision

D) To match the uniform

135. Agreement and Sentence Structure:

Which of the following sentences is grammatically correct?

A) The dogs chases the cat.

B) The dogs chase the cat.

C) The dog chase the cat.

D) The dogs chases the cats.

136. Chemistry:

Which of the following is NOT a noble gas?

A) Helium

B) Neon

C) Chlorine

D) Argon

137. Foundations of Grammar:

Identify the verb in the following sentence: "The cat slept on the mat."

A) Cat

B) On

C) The

D) Slept

138. Geology:

What type of rock is formed by the alteration of pre-existing rock deep within Earth's crust?

A) Sedimentary

B) Igneous

C) Metamorphic

D) None of the above

139. Reading Comprehension:

If a passage describes the consequences of deforestation, what is likely the author's main purpose?

A) To entertain

B) To persuade

C) To inform

D) To argue

140. Biology:

Which part of a plant cell is responsible for photosynthesis?

A) Nucleus

B) Mitochondria

C) Ribosomes

D) Chloroplasts

141. Physics:

What is the acceleration due to gravity at the Earth's surface?

A) 9.8 m/s^2

B) 8.9 m/s^2

C) 10 m/s^2

D) 7.8 m/s^2

142. Social Studies Skills and Pedagogy:

Which skill is essential for historians to analyze primary sources?

A) Calculating

B) Critical thinking

C) Memorizing

D) Painting

143. Two-Dimensional Shapes:

Which of the following shapes has no parallel sides?

A) Rectangle

B) Square

C) Rhombus

D) Trapezoid

144. Literary Analysis:

In literature, what does a metaphor do?

A) Compares two things without using "like" or "as"

B) Compares two things using "like" or "as"

C) Describes a sound

D) Provides a detailed setting

145. World History:

Who was the last emperor of the French before the establishment of the French Third Republic?

A) Napoleon Bonaparte

B) Louis XVIII

C) Charles X

D) Napoleon III

146. Probability:

What is the probability of drawing an Ace from a standard deck of 52 playing cards?

A) 1/13

B) 1/4

C) 1/52

D) 4/52

147. Civics and Citizenship:

Which amendment to the U.S. Constitution gave women the right to vote?

A) 19th Amendment

B) 15th Amendment

C) 21st Amendment

D) 13th Amendment

148. Equations:

Which of the following is a linear equation?

A) $y=2x^2+3$

B) $3x+4y=10$

C) $|x|=5$

D) $2^x=16$

149. Economics:

What is fiscal policy primarily concerned with?

A) Government spending and taxation

B) Supply and demand

C) International trade

D) Monetary supply

150. Vocabulary and Word Relationships:

Which word is antonymous with "antagonize"?

A) Harass

B) Irritate

C) Soothe

D) Provoke

151. Chemistry:

What is the chemical formula for sulfur dioxide?

A) SO

B) SO_2

C) S_2O

D) S_2O_3

152. Reading Comprehension:

What is the main purpose of a conclusion in an essay?

A) To introduce the topic

B) To provide evidence

C) To summarize the main points

D) To ask questions

153. Biology:

What is the process by which plants convert light energy into chemical energy?

A) Respiration

B) Digestion

C) Photosynthesis

D) Fermentation

154. Advanced Functions:

If $f(x)=3x^2-2x+4$, what is the value of $f(2)$?

A) 16

B) 12

C) 14

D) 18

155. Geography:

What is the capital of Japan?

A) Kyoto

B) Osaka

C) Tokyo

D) Nagasaki

156. U.S. History:

What event significantly contributed to the start of the American Revolutionary War?

A) The signing of the Constitution

B) The Emancipation Proclamation

C) The Boston Tea Party

D) The Louisiana Purchase

157. Inequalities:

Which inequality is represented by the graph showing all points to the right of $x=3$?

A) $x<3$

B) $x\leq3$

C) $x>3$

D) $x\geq3$

158. Foundations of Grammar:

Identify the subject in the following sentence: "The cat chased the mouse."

A) The mouse

B) Chased

C) The cat

D) Mouse

159. Punctuation:

What is the correct punctuation for the following sentence: "She said 'Good morning John' "?

A) "She said, 'Good morning, John.'"

B) "She said, Good morning, John."

C) "She said 'Good morning, John'."

D) "She said 'Good morning John'."

160. Basic Functions:

What is the quadratic formula used to solve?

A) Linear equations

B) Quadratic equations

C) Cubic equations

D) Exponential equations

161. ELA Pedagogy:

Which of the following strategies is most effective for teaching reading comprehension to elementary students?

A) Lecturing on literary history

B) Teaching phonics and vocabulary

C) Assigning silent reading without guidance

D) Focusing solely on spelling

162. Rational Numbers:

What is the sum of −1/3 and 5/6?

A) 2/3

B) 1/6

C) 1/2

D) 1/3

163. Geology:

What geological process is responsible for the formation of mountains through the collision of tectonic plates?

A) Weathering

B) Erosion

C) Subduction

D) Orogeny

164. U.S. Government:

Which branch of the U.S. government is responsible for interpreting the Constitution?

A) Executive

B) Legislative

C) Judicial

D) Administrative

165. Scientific Inquiry and Lab Safety:

What should you do if a chemical spills on your skin during a lab experiment?

A) Ignore it

B) Wash the affected area with water

C) Call a friend

D) Taste it to identify the chemical

166. Science, Technology, and Society:

Which invention had the greatest impact on communication in the 20th century?

A) Printing press

B) Internet

C) Steam engine

D) Light bulb

167. Agreement and Sentence Structure:

Which sentence is grammatically correct?

A) Him and I went to the store.

B) He and me went to the store.

C) He and I went to the store.

D) Me and him went to the store.

168. Economics:

What economic system is characterized by government control of all major economic decisions?

A) Capitalism

B) Socialism

C) Command Economy

D) Mixed Economy

169. Literary Analysis:

What is the term for the time and place of a story's action?

A) Theme

B) Plot

C) Setting

D) Character

170. Statistics and Probability:

If you draw two cards without replacement from a standard deck of 52 cards, what is the probability that both cards are spades?

A) 1/26

B) 1/17

C) 1/13

D) 1/17

171. Two-Dimensional Shapes:

What is the sum of the interior angles of a triangle?

A) 90 degrees

B) 120 degrees

C) 180 degrees

D) 360 degrees

172. World History:

Which Chinese emperor is known for the construction of the Great Wall of China?

A) Qin Shi Huang

B) Han Wudi

C) Emperor Wu of Jin

D) Emperor Taizong of Tang

173. Chemistry:

Which element is represented by the chemical symbol K?

A) Potassium

B) Krypton

C) Kryptonite

D) Potash

174. Physics:

What is the force exerted on a 5 kg object accelerating at 2 m/s^2?

A) 10 N

B) 7 N

C) 2 N

D) 25 N

175. Reading Comprehension:

In the statement "The early bird catches the worm," what is implied?

A) Worms are easily caught

B) Birds eat early

C) Success comes to those who prepare early

D) All birds eat worms

176. Civics and Citizenship:

Which U.S. Constitutional amendment guarantees freedom of speech?

A) First Amendment

B) Second Amendment

C) Fifth Amendment

D) Tenth Amendment

177. Advanced Functions:

What is the asymptote of the function $h(x)=1/x-3$?

A) $x=3$

B) $y=0$

C) $y=3$

D) $x=0$

178. Geography:

Which river is the longest in the world?

A) Amazon River

B) Nile River

C) Yangtze River

D) Mississippi River

179. U.S. Government:

How many justices serve on the United States Supreme Court?

A) 9

B) 7

C) 11

D) 13

180. Vocabulary and Word Relationships:

Choose the synonym for "elaborate."

A) Simple

B) Basic

C) Complex

D) Plain

181. Agreement and Sentence Structure:

Which sentence is correct?

A) Each of the students have a book.

B) Each of the students has a book.

C) Neither of the students have a book.

D) Neither of the students has books.

182. Economics:

What is the term for a market with many buyers and sellers, none of whom can influence the price?

A) Monopoly

B) Oligopoly

C) Perfect Competition

D) Monopolistic Competition

183. Literary Analysis:

What literary device is used to give human characteristics to non-human objects?

A) Alliteration

B) Onomatopoeia

C) Personification

D) Simile

184. Probability:

If you roll a fair six-sided die, what is the probability of rolling a number less than 5?

A) 2/3

B) 3/4

C) 1/2

D) 2/6

185. Biology:

What is the term for the opening and closing of small pores on the surface of leaves, regulating gas exchange and water loss in plants?

A) Stomata

B) Chloroplasts

C) Xylem

D) Phloem

186. Basic Functions:

What is the period of the function $k(x)=\sin(2x)$?

A) π

B) 2π

C) $\pi/2$

D) $\pi/4$

187. U.S. History:

Who was the third President of the United States?

A) John Adams

B) Thomas Jefferson

C) George Washington

D) James Madison

188. Scientific Inquiry and Lab Safety:

What should always be worn to protect the eyes during a laboratory experiment?

A) Gloves

B) Safety goggles

C) Lab coat

D) Earplugs

189. Two-Dimensional Shapes:

What is the term for a four-sided polygon with opposite sides equal and parallel, and all angles equal to 90 degrees?

A) Square

B) Rhombus

C) Rectangle

D) Parallelogram

190. Equations:

Solve the equation $4(x-3)=8$.

A) $x=2$

B) $x=3$

C) $x=5$

D) $x=6$

191. Geology:

What is the process by which rocks are broken down into smaller particles due to weathering and erosion?

A) Lithification

B) Metamorphism

C) Deposition

D) Mechanical weathering

192. Punctuation:

Which sentence is punctuated correctly?

A) The dogs, tail was wagging.

B) The dog's tail, was wagging.

C) The dogs' tail was wagging.

D) The dog's tail was wagging.

193. Science, Technology, and Society:

What scientist is best known for his theory of relativity?

A) Isaac Newton

B) Charles Darwin

C) Albert Einstein

D) Nikola Tesla

194. Inequalities:

If $2x+3<9$, what is the maximum integer value of x?

A) 2

B) 1

C) 3

D) 0

195. Chemistry:

What type of bond is formed when electrons are shared between atoms?

A) Ionic

B) Metallic

C) Covalent

D) Hydrogen

196. Physics:

What is the term for the amount of matter in an object?

A) Weight

B) Mass

C) Volume

D) Density

197. Vocabulary and Word Relationships:

What is the antonym of "courageous"?

A) Timid

B) Confident

C) Fearless

D) Brave

198. Social Studies Skills and Pedagogy:

What teaching strategy emphasizes understanding and applying concepts instead of rote memorization?

A) Drill and practice

B) Inquiry-based learning

C) Lecturing

D) Role-playing

199. Literary Analysis:

What is the climax of a story?

A) The beginning

B) The resolution

C) The turning point

D) The introduction of characters

200. Rational Numbers:

What is the product of 2/3 and its reciprocal?

A) 0

B) 1

C) 2/3

D) 2

6.2 Answer Sheet - Practice Test 2

101. Answer: C

Explanation: Safety goggles should always be worn during a lab experiment to protect the eyes.

102. Answer: D

Explanation: The probability of getting heads on a single flip is 1/2. Since the events are independent, the probability of getting heads on two consecutive flips is (1/2) * (1/2) = 1/4.

103. Answer: A

Explanation: The perimeter of a rectangle is given by 2×(length+width)=2×(8+4)=24 units.

104. Answer: D

Explanation: $4x-5=11 \Rightarrow 4x=16 \Rightarrow x=4$.

105. Answer: B

Explanation: Augustus Caesar was the first Emperor of the Roman Empire.

106. Answer: C

Explanation: The main duty of the judicial branch is to interpret laws.

107. Answer: A

Explanation: The SI unit of luminous intensity is the candela.

108. Answer: B

- **Explanation**: The chemical symbol for sodium is Na.

109. Answer: A

Explanation: Dividing both sides by 5, we get $x<3$.

110. Answer: A

Explanation: The derivative of the given function is $6x-2$.

111. Answer: A

Explanation: This phrase is a metaphor, comparing time to something that can fly.

112. Answer: B

Explanation: The law of supply states that, all else being equal, an increase in price results in an increase in the quantity supplied.

113. Answer: D

Explanation: The inner core is primarily composed of solid iron and nickel.

114. Answer: C

Explanation: Geothermal energy derives power from the heat stored in Earth's interior.

115. Answer: A

Explanation: The slope of a horizontal line is 0 because the line does not rise or fall; it is parallel to the x-axis.

116. Answer: A

Explanation: To add fractions, find a common denominator. In this case, the common denominator is 6. So, 5/2+1/3=15/6+2/6=17/6, which simplifies to 11/6.

117. Answer: A

Explanation: The First Amendment to the U.S. Constitution guarantees freedom of speech.

118. Answer: A

Explanation: The acceleration due to gravity on the surface of the Earth is 9.8 m/s^2.

119. Answer: C

Explanation: The main cause of the American Revolutionary War was taxation without representation.

120. Answer: B

Explanation: The atomic number of an element represents the total number of protons in the nucleus of an atom.

121. Answer: B

Explanation: A semicolon is used to separate two closely related independent clauses.

122. Answer: D

Explanation: The capital city of France is Paris.

123. Answer: B

Explanation: The liver is responsible for detoxification in the human body.

124. Answer: C

Explanation: Solving for x, we have $5x=15$, so $x=3$.

125. Answer: C

Explanation: The theme in literature refers to the central idea or message.

126. Answer: A

Explanation: Margaret Thatcher was the first female Prime Minister of the United Kingdom.

127. Answer: B

Explanation: The inequality "five times a number is at least 15" is represented by $5x \geq 15$.

128. Answer: C

Explanation: The minimum age requirement to become President of the United States is 35.

129. Answer: A

Explanation: The area of a triangle is given by $1/2 \times base \times height = 1/2 \times 10 \times 5 = 25$ square units.

130. Answer: B

Explanation: "Ubiquitous" means present everywhere, so the synonym is "Common."

131. Answer: B

Explanation: A market economy is primarily guided by supply and demand.

132. Answer: B

Explanation: $f(-1)=(-1)^2+2(-1)-3=1-2-3=-5+1=-4$.

133. Answer: C

Explanation: There are two numbers greater than 4 (5 and 6) out of a total of six possible outcomes, so the probability is 2/6, which simplifies to 1/6.

134. Answer: B

Explanation: Safety goggles are worn in a laboratory setting to protect the eyes from harmful chemicals or objects.

135. Answer: B

Explanation: The correct sentence is "The dogs chase the cat," as it maintains subject-verb agreement.

136. Answer: C

Explanation: Chlorine is not a noble gas; it is a halogen.

137. Answer: D

Explanation: The verb in the sentence is "slept."

138. Answer: C

Explanation: Metamorphic rock is formed by the alteration of pre-existing rock deep within Earth's crust.

139. Answer: C

Explanation: The author's main purpose in describing the consequences of deforestation is likely to inform.

140. Answer: D

Explanation: Chloroplasts are the part of a plant cell responsible for photosynthesis.

141. Answer: A

Explanation: The acceleration due to gravity at the Earth's surface is 9.8 m/s^2.

142. Answer: B

Explanation: Critical thinking is essential for historians to analyze primary sources.

143. Answer: C

Explanation: A rhombus may have equal sides, but it does not necessarily have parallel sides.

144. Answer: A

Explanation: A metaphor compares two things without using "like" or "as."

145. Answer: D

Explanation: Napoleon III, nephew of Napoleon Bonaparte, served as the last monarch and the final emperor of the French before the establishment of the French Third Republic.

146. Answer: D

Explanation: There are 4 Aces in a standard deck of 52 playing cards, so the probability is 4/52.

147. Answer: A

Explanation: The 19th Amendment to the U.S. Constitution gave women the right to vote.

148. Answer: B

Explanation: A linear equation is of the form *ax+by=c*, and option B fits this form.

149. Answer: A

Explanation: Fiscal policy is primarily concerned with government spending and taxation.

150. Answer: C

Explanation: "Antagonize" means to cause someone to become hostile, so the antonym is "soothe."

151. Answer: B

Explanation: The chemical formula for sulfur dioxide is SO2.

152. Answer: C

Explanation: The main purpose of a conclusion in an essay is to summarize the main points.

153. Answer: C

Explanation: The process by which plants convert light energy into chemical energy is photosynthesis.

154. Answer: B

Explanation: $f(2)=3\times 2^2-2\times 2+4=12-4+4=12$.

155. Answer: C

Explanation: The capital of Japan is Tokyo.

156. Answer: C

Explanation: The Boston Tea Party significantly contributed to the start of the American Revolutionary War.

157. Answer: C

Explanation: The graph showing all points to the right of $x=3$ represents the inequality $x>3$.

158. Answer: C

Explanation: In the sentence, "The cat chased the mouse," the subject is "The cat."

159. Answer: A

Explanation: The correct punctuation is: "She said, 'Good morning, John.'"

160. Answer: B

Explanation: The quadratic formula $x=\frac{-b\pm\sqrt{b^2-4ac}}{2a}$ is used to find solutions for quadratic equations in the form $ax^2+bx+c=0$.

161. Answer: B

Explanation: Teaching phonics and vocabulary is the most effective strategy for teaching reading comprehension to elementary students.

162. Answer: B

Explanation: The sum of −1/3 and 5/6 is 1/6.

163. Answer: D

Explanation: Orogeny is the geological process that leads to the formation of mountains through the collision of tectonic plates.

164. Answer: C

Explanation: The Judicial branch of the U.S. government is responsible for interpreting the Constitution.

165. Answer: B

Explanation: If a chemical spills on your skin during a lab experiment, you should wash the affected area with water.

166. Answer: B

Explanation: The invention of the Internet had the greatest impact on communication in the 20th century.

167. Answer: C

Explanation: The grammatically correct sentence is: "He and I went to the store."

168. Answer: C

Explanation: A command economy is characterized by government control of all major economic decisions.

169. Answer: C

Explanation: The term for the time and place of a story's action is the setting.

170. Answer: B

Explanation: After drawing the first spade, there are 12 spades left out of a total of 51 cards. Therefore, the probability of drawing a second spade is 12/51, which simplifies to 4/17. The probability of both events occurring is (1/4) * (4/17) = 1/17.

171. Answer: C

Explanation: The sum of the interior angles of any triangle is always 180 degrees.

172. Answer: A

Explanation: Qin Shi Huang, the first emperor of the Qin Dynasty, is renowned for ordering the construction of the Great Wall of China.

173. Answer: A

Explanation: The chemical symbol for potassium is K.

174. Answer: A

Explanation: The force exerted can be calculated using the equation $F=ma=5kg \times 2m/s^2=10N$.

175. Answer: C

Explanation: The statement implies that success comes to those who prepare early.

176. Answer: A

Explanation: The First Amendment to the U.S. Constitution guarantees freedom of speech.

177. Answer: A) $x=3$

Explanation: The function $h(x)=1/x-3$ has a vertical asymptote at $x=3$.

178. Answer: B

Explanation: The Nile River is generally recognized as the longest river in the world.

179. Answer: A

Explanation: There are 9 justices who serve on the United States Supreme Court.

180. Answer: C

Explanation: "Elaborate" and "complex" both suggest intricacy and detailed design.

181. Answer: B

Explanation: The correct sentence is "Each of the students has a book."

182. Answer: C

Explanation: The term for a market with many buyers and sellers, none of whom can influence the price, is Perfect Competition.

183. Answer: C

Explanation: Personification is the literary device used to give human characteristics to non-human objects.

184. Answer: A

Explanation: There are four numbers less than 5 (1, 2, 3, 4) out of a total of six possible outcomes, so the probability is 4/6, which simplifies to 2/3.

185. Answer: A

Explanation: Stomata are small pores on the surface of leaves that open and close to regulate gas exchange (including CO_2 intake for photosynthesis) and water loss.

186. Answer: B) 2π

Explanation: The period of $k(x)=\sin(2x)$ is given by 2π because the coefficient of x inside the sine function affects the period.

187. Answer: B

Explanation: Thomas Jefferson was the third President of the United States.

188. Answer: B

Explanation: Safety goggles should always be worn to protect the eyes during a laboratory experiment.

189. Answer: A

Explanation: A square is a four-sided polygon with equal and parallel sides and all angles equal to 90 degrees.

190. Answer: C) $x=5$

Explanation: Distribute 4, then solve for x: $4x-12=8 \square 4x=20 \square x=5$.

191. Answer: D

Explanation: Mechanical weathering is the process by which rocks are broken down into smaller particles.

192. Answer: D

Explanation: The correct punctuation is "The dog's tail was wagging."

193. Answer: C

Explanation: Albert Einstein is best known for his theory of relativity.

194. Answer: A

Explanation: Solving the inequality, $2x+3<9 \Rightarrow 2x<6 \Rightarrow x<3$, so the maximum integer value of x is 2.

195. Answer: C

Explanation: Covalent bonds are formed when electrons are shared between atoms.

196. Answer: B

Explanation: Mass is the term for the amount of matter in an object.

197. Answer: A

Explanation: "Courageous" and "Timid" are antonyms, as they represent opposite qualities related to bravery.

198. Answer: B

Explanation: Inquiry-based learning emphasizes understanding and applying concepts instead of rote memorization.

199. Answer: C

Explanation: The climax of a story is the turning point, where the main conflict reaches its peak.

200. Answer: B

Explanation: The product of a number and its reciprocal is always 1.

Test-Taking Strategies

Succeeding in the FTCE Elementary Education K-6 exam requires not only content mastery but also strategic test-taking skills. Here are some proven strategies:

1. **Read the Instructions Carefully**: Before starting, ensure you understand the directions, question formats, and scoring rules.

2. **Pace Yourself**: With time constraints, it's essential to divide your time wisely. If a question seems too tricky, move on and return to it later.

3. **Eliminate Wrong Answers**: If you're unsure about a multiple-choice question, eliminate improbable options, then make an educated guess.

4. **Mark and Review**: Utilize any feature that allows you to flag questions for review. Revisit them if time permits.

5. **Use All Available Time**: Don't rush. If you finish early, review your answers and make sure you haven't skipped anything.

6. **Trust Your Preparation**: Remember, this guide has prepared you thoroughly, so trust your knowledge and judgment.

Overcoming Test Anxiety

Test anxiety is common but can be managed with these strategies:

1. **Preparation**: Knowing that you've prepared adequately will boost your confidence. Follow the study schedules and practice tests in this guide.

2. **Relaxation Techniques**: Practice deep breathing or visualization techniques to calm your nerves.

3. **Positive Reinforcement**: Encourage yourself with positive affirmations and remember past successes.

4. **Know What to Expect**: Familiarize yourself with the test format, rules, and location beforehand. A "dry run" to the test center might ease anxiety about logistics.

5. **Eat and Sleep Well**: Ensure a balanced diet and adequate rest leading up to the exam day. A well-nourished and rested mind performs better.

6. **Seek Support if Needed**: If anxiety becomes overwhelming, consider seeking support from friends, family, or professionals.

Conclusion:

Test-taking strategies and managing anxiety are vital components of a successful exam experience. Embrace the strategies outlined here and incorporate them into your practice sessions.

Remember, Test Treasure Publication's commitment to personalized learning means we are with you every step of the way. Our guidance transcends mere exam preparation; we aim to empower you with the skills and confidence needed not just for this exam but for a future filled with extraordinary possibilities.

Believe in yourself, and embrace this journey with determination, resilience, and an unyielding pursuit of excellence.

Additional Resources

The journey towards acing the FTCE Elementary Education K-6 exam isn't limited to this study guide alone. To enhance your understanding and practice, we recommend the following online resources and academic materials.

Recommended Online Resources

1. **Florida Department of Education FTCE Page**: The official website offers essential information, including registration, test dates, and official study materials.

2. **Educational Forums and Communities**: Platforms like TeachersPayTeachers and Reddit's teaching communities can offer peer support, share experiences, and provide additional resources.

3. **Khan Academy**: Excellent for brushing up on Math, Science, and Language Arts concepts, Khan Academy offers free video tutorials and practice exercises.

4. **YouTube Education Channels**: Many educators offer subject-specific tutorials, strategies, and insights through YouTube.

5. **Quizlet**: Create or find flashcard sets specific to FTCE Elementary Education K-6 topics for memorization and quick review.

Recommended Academic Materials

1. **Florida State-Adopted Textbooks**: These provide comprehensive coverage of the state's standards and guidelines for K-6 education.

2. **National Council for the Social Studies (NCSS) Publications**: For an in-depth understanding of Social Science topics.

3. **National Science Teachers Association (NSTA) Books**: These resources are tailored to Science educators and cover essential content aligned with the exam.

4. **NCTM Publications**: The National Council of Teachers of Mathematics provides materials focusing on effective Mathematics teaching strategies.

5. **Local Libraries and University Resources**: Consider accessing the education sections of local libraries or nearby universities for scholarly articles, educational journals, and additional textbooks.

Conclusion

These resources are meant to complement the comprehensive guidance provided by Test Treasure Publishing's FTCE Elementary Education K-6 Study Guide. We encourage you to explore them as you tailor your study plan to your unique learning style and needs.

While this guide remains your primary mentor, supplementing it with these additional resources will further deepen your understanding and sharpen your skills. As always, our goal is to illuminate your path to extraordinary success, one step at a time.

EXPLORE OUR RANGE OF STUDY GUIDES

At Test Treasure Publication, we understand that academic success requires more than just raw intelligence or tireless effort—it requires targeted preparation. That's why we offer an extensive range of study guides, meticulously designed to help you excel in various exams across the USA.

Our Offerings

- **Medical Exams:** Conquer the MCAT, USMLE, and more with our comprehensive study guides, complete with practice questions and diagnostic tests.

- **Law Exams:** Get a leg up on the LSAT and bar exams with our tailored resources, offering theoretical insights and practical exercises.

- **Business and Management Tests:** Ace the GMAT and other business exams with our incisive guides, equipped with real-world examples and scenarios.

- **Engineering & Technical Exams:** Prep for the FE, PE, and other technical exams with our specialized guides, which delve into both fundamentals and complexities.

- **High School Exams:** Be it the SAT, ACT, or AP tests, our high school range is designed to give you a competitive edge.

- **State-Specific Exams:** Tailored resources to help you with exams unique to specific states, whether it's teacher qualification exams or state civil service exams.

Why Choose Test Treasure Publication?

- **Comprehensive Coverage:** Each guide covers all essential topics in detail.

- **Quality Material:** Crafted by experts in each field.

- **Interactive Tools:** Flashcards, online quizzes, and downloadable resources to complement your study.

- **Customizable Learning:** Personalize your prep journey by focusing on areas where you need the most help.

- **Community Support:** Access to online forums where you can discuss concerns, seek guidance, and share success stories.

Contact Us

For inquiries about our study guides, or to provide feedback, please email us at support@testtreasure.com.

Order Now

Ready to elevate your preparation to the next level? Visit our website www.testtreasure.com to browse our complete range of study guides and make your purchase.